"Not Charity, but Justice"

"Not Charity, but Justice"

The Story of

JACOB A. RIIS

by Edith
Patterson
Meyer

*The Vanguard
Press, Inc.
New York*

To My Nephews

BRIANT *and* JOHN

Contents

Contents

Photographs

BY JACOB A. RIIS

*By courtesy of The Jacob A. Riis Collection,
Museum of the City of New York*

Acknowledgments Besides consulting books in the New York Public Library and in the Ferguson Library of Stamford, Connecticut, I made much use of the old magazine files in the Ferguson Library and also in the Pequot Library of Southport, Connecticut. At the Museum of the City of New York, Miss Charlotte LaRue, librarian, introduced me to the collection of Jacob Riis documentary photographs. In the Manuscripts and Archives Division of the New York Public Library I went over hundreds of letters and notes of Jacob Riis, from some of which I have quoted directly by consent of Mr. Riis's grandson, Mr. J. Riis Owre of Coral Gables, Florida, and Mr. John P. Baker, then Executive Assistant, The Research Libraries, New York Public Library. Mr. James Sullivan, librarian of the Barre, Massachusetts, Public Library, made available old local newspapers, and at the Barre Historical Society Mrs. C. S. Connington produced other relevant printed matter, and also took me to the "God's Acre" where an uninscribed boulder marks Jacob Riis's grave.

I thank most warmly all these gracious, cooperative persons, as well as the many others who assisted me in my search for Riis material.

Author's Note   Most of my source material on Jacob
Riis I found in his own writings, for he revealed a great
deal about himself in whatever subject he wrote on.
Through his own words one can see him first as an impulsive young Dane, then as an enthusiastic American
untiring in his battle to better the intolerable living and
working conditions of the very poor. His ideas made
their mark and influenced the direction taken by social
reform all over America. Some of those ideas may now
seem oversimple, but many are still being followed.

Not long ago I took the "fairyland" tour of Denmark.
On a narrow cobblestoned street in Jacob Riis's native
town our young lady guide pointed to a bronze plaque
set on a row of attached brick houses to mark the birth-
place of Jacob Riis. Most of us were Americans, yet almost everyone looked blank. As the guide started to move
on a young New York lawyer spoke up. "Have none of
you ever heard of Jacob Riis?" he asked unbelievingly.
"Then you should learn a little about him."

Ignoring the guide's restlessness, the young man told
briefly of the young immigrant from Ribe who became a
New York police reporter and was so horrified at what
he saw while investigating crime in the slum district that

he spent his life writing, lecturing, and working to better the living conditions of the poor. So effectively did he awaken New York's social conscience that its citizens compelled the city and state to improve housing, build schools and parks and playgrounds, and eliminate sweatshops and child labor. "Jacob Riis," the young lawyer ended his little talk, "was the one who really got social reform going in New York and pushed it ahead all over America."

As the guide led us on down the street we were thoughtfully silent, impressed by the enthusiastic unscheduled speech. This incident was one of the sparks that kindled the writing of this book.

*"Not
Charity,
but
Justice"*

I

Stranger
in
a New Land

"Nothing in all this world is without
a purpose."
—*The Making of an American*

Imagine a young man strolling up New York's Broadway,
looking sharply to right and left. He is not a large man,
but he looks strong and there is something attractive
about his rather boyish face. A heavy revolver swings
from his belt and his clothes are far from modish. The
time is June, 1870, and the young man is Jacob August
Riis, aged twenty-one, just arrived from Denmark to seek
his fortune in America. His trunk has gone to a Danish
rooming house on Battery Place and he has made his first
purchase—the revolver. It cost him exactly half the forty
dollars that was his complete stock of money, but he is
sure it was money well spent and that he will soon have
need of it.

In his home town of Ribe, Denmark, Jacob had read
stories of America. He read them in English—a language
he learned at school and from his teacher father. His
favorites among them were the Indian tales written by
James Fenimore Cooper, and from them he had drawn

his idea of America. It was, he believed, a land full of Indians, wigwams, buffaloes and other wild animals. A drawing in a picture book he had seen as a little boy had made an impression too. It showed sleighs racing along through wild, snowy country, bound, Jacob imagined, for a buffalo hunt—or perhaps they were heading toward an Indian ambush!

Now Jacob discovered that New York was a busy city, with its streets "actually paved, with no buffaloes in sight and not a red man or a beaver hut." To his astonishment, it looked more like Denmark's capital city of Copenhagen than a scene described by Cooper. A kindly policeman came up and tapped the revolver with his club. He assured the young immigrant he would not be needing the weapon in New York and suggested he put it out of sight. Since it was uncomfortably heavy as well as unnecessary, Jacob was glad to stow it away in his trunk when he returned to his boardinghouse.

Young Riis carried letters of introduction to the Danish consul and to a businessman acquaintance of his family. Both of them were away, so he set out on his own to find work and for several days searched for a job. He had no luck and he began to wonder if making his fortune in America was going to be as simple as he had imagined. Where was this "golden land of opportunity" he had heard so much about?

Jacob was a skilled carpenter, for he had dropped out of school and become a carpenter's apprentice, to the disappointment of his father, who was a senior master in the Ribe Latin school. But the young immigrant was "tired of the hammer and saw" and sure there must be quicker ways to succeed in this new land. To become successful was important to him, for he intended to go back to Denmark and win for his wife the pretty Ribe girl, Elisabeth, he still thought of as his sweetheart in spite of her having turned him down.

It was a bad year in New York. No one seemed to need Jacob Riis's services, even as a carpenter. The city—with its sharp contrast of rich and poor, the rough-and-tumble men fiercely fighting one another for jobs, the dirty and disorderly downtown streets—on closer inspection looked very different from clean, orderly Copenhagen. Bewildered and disappointed, Jacob came across a gang of men whose railroad fare was being paid to a coal mine and iron works in western Pennsylvania where they had agreed to work, and he decided to go with them.

There, because of his skill as a carpenter, he was given the job of building huts for the coal miners to live in. But he was curious about mining and wanted to see what it was like, so he tried it. One day was enough. He hated being underground and he found the mine so dark and dangerous and the work of digging coal with a pick so hard and dirty that he was glad to go back to carpentering.

The hilly country of western Pennsylvania was very different from the flat land of Denmark. Jacob did not like it and he was homesick. He heard of a war going on between France and Germany, Denmark's ancient enemy, and he was sure that a Danish troop would be formed in New York and sent across the Atlantic to fight against Germany. If he joined it and won fame and glory in the war, he might return to Ribe as a gallant soldier. Then surely he would be able to persuade Elisabeth to change her mind and could also overcome her foster parents' ob-

3

jection to their daughter's marrying a common carpenter. Filled with this dream, Jacob quit his job and headed for New York to enlist. His wages took him only as far as Buffalo, so there he pawned his trunk with most of its contents for enough money to buy a ticket to New York.

At the Danish consulate young Riis was told there was no arrangement for free passage to Europe for fighters in the Franco-German War. His name would be set down, they said, in case the situation changed. Bitterly disappointed, Jacob walked away. He had pawned his revolver and top boots to pay for his night's lodging and was completely out of money. Aimlessly walking northward through the city, he stopped to rest on the Fordham University campus. He accepted food from a friendly priest, then went on his way. For several days he earned his meals by doing odd jobs at farms in the nearby countryside. At night he slept in the fields. It was full summer and he enjoyed being out of doors.

Still clinging to the idea of becoming a soldier, he read in the *New York Sun* an item about a volunteer regiment being fitted out for France, and headed back to the downtown part of the city. In the office of the *Sun* he talked to its noted editor, Charles A. Dana. Mr. Dana told him he knew nothing about the matter and strongly advised him to forget the whole idea. But when the editor pulled a dollar bill from his pocket and offered it to him, suggesting he get himself a good meal, Jacob haughtily refused the money. "I came here to enlist, not to beg money for breakfast," he said.

Hungry and again frustrated, Jacob left the city once more, this time heading south. In New Jersey he found

4

work in a brickyard. He stayed there for six weeks, although he did not get on very well with the other employees, most of whom were German and who teased him by celebrating each victory the Germans won over the French in the European war. Riis's job was to walk alongside a big white horse hitched to a cart loaded with clay, back the cart up to the clay pit, and dump the load into the pit.

One day, dreaming about Elisabeth, he forgot to take out the cart's tailboard when he tilted the cart up; the weight of the load dragged cart, clay, and horse backward into the pit. Things had a way of striking Jacob Riis as funny, and the sight of the upended white horse, its four legs pointing skyward, struck him as so ridiculous that he sat on the edge of the pit and howled with laughter. Men who had seen the accident came running to pull the horse out of the pit. When they sawed the bent shaft apart, it rebounded and hit one of the workers in the head, knocking him senseless. Things did not look so funny then to Jacob. For an hour, until the unconscious worker recovered, he was a very worried young man. He thought he would surely be fired, but instead he was demoted to the job of pushing a cart loaded with bricks. Luckily he was a strong fellow, for it was hard work.

When Jacob, still smitten with the war fever, heard of a company of volunteers about to sail for France, he drew his pay, left the brickyard, and went back to New York. To his dismay he was too late; the company had already sailed. He called at the French consulate, then called again—and again—so often that he became a nuisance and was finally ordered out in no uncertain terms. This made the would-be volunteer so angry that he struck the French consul, who struck back. Horrified clerks came running as the two angry men tumbled down the carpeted stairs, pummeling and clawing at each other. The clerks disentangled them and threw Riis out into the street. He picked himself up, wiped away a streak of blood from his cheek, and looked about with an eye that was beginning to swell. Then he laughed, consoled by the thought that in a few hours the French consul, too, would have a beautiful black eye.

Riis's brickyard wages were soon gone, along with his dream of becoming a soldier. His trunk, which he had now recovered, he had to leave at his boardinghouse as security. Once again he set out looking for work. There was no point in returning to the New Jersey brickyard, for the weather was getting too cold for brickmaking. Although he had, as he later said, "a pair of strong hands and stubbornness enough to do for two," these did not seem to be of any use to him now. Many other men were, like him, roaming the streets in search of jobs that simply did not exist. Proud, Jacob refused to beg, as he saw many of them doing. He tore up the two letters of introduction he still carried so that he would not be tempted to call on his family's friends in his shabby condition. But he did not go too hungry, for each night, at a back window of Delmonico's elegant restaurant, a French-speaking chef with whom he had made friends handed him a full plate. This Riis considered not begging, but an act of friendship. Lodging was a more difficult problem. The sheltered doorways of the lower part of Manhattan became familiar

6

to him. So did the words: "Get up! Move on!" accompanied by the prod of a policeman's boot or club.

In these discouraging days and nights of wandering about, looking unsuccessfully for work, young Riis grew well acquainted with the Mulberry Street neighborhood of lower New York. As he walked up and down the poverty-stricken streets he had no idea they would later be the scene of his working life for many years. Nor did he dream that his sufferings and the firsthand knowledge he was gaining as a homeless immigrant would one day be helpful to him in understanding and trying to relieve the problems of New York's foreign-born poor.

The nights were getting colder, the fall rains chilly, and Jacob's clothes were worn thin. One cold rainy night he sat on a river pier, soaked through and shivering. Discouraged beyond hope, he looked at the dark water and began to wonder about the use of going on. A small black and tan dog crept up beside him, whined, nuzzled him, and licked his face. This affectionate canine companionship brought Jacob to his senses and restored his natural optimism. He tucked the little dog under his arm, got to his feet, and set out once more in the unfriendly world.

For the first time Jacob sought refuge in a police-station lodging-room. These shelters for vagrants were little more than bare rooms with filthy planks for beds, where the bedmaking task consisted merely of turning the planks! In spite of Riis's pleading, the little dog was not allowed inside and took up its post on the steps outside the door.

The lodging-room was jammed with tramps. When one of them talked loudly about the European war, strongly favoring the Germans, Riis could not keep silent and spoke up for the other side. The argument became so heated that the policeman in charge threatened to lock them all up if they did not quiet down. At last Riis, like most of the others, fell into an uneasy sleep.

During the night a tramp managed to steal a gold locket that Jacob had kept in spite of hunger and want and that he wore on a string around his neck. Terribly upset when he discovered the theft, he reported it to the desk sergeant, who did not believe him. How would a tramp have a gold locket? Unless, of course, he had stolen it, in which case he should be locked up. Provoked beyond reason, Riis lost his temper and talked back. The sergeant called the doorman and ordered the unruly fellow thrown out.

On the police-station steps sat the little dog. It had been waiting for its master all night and now, seeing him roughly handled, it sprang toward the police doorman and fastened its teeth in his leg. With a howl the angry man picked up the little dog and before Riis's horrified eyes beat its brains out against the stone steps. Wild with rage, Riis gathered loose paving stones from the gutter and flung them toward the police station. The sergeant, hearing the commotion, appeared. He sensed that things had gone too far and ordered two policemen to march the maniac out of their precinct.

Riis could not get out of the neighborhood or out of New York quickly enough. Never, he swore, would he forget this act; someday, he vowed, he would have his revenge. Overflowing with rage and bitterness, ragged, penniless, and hungry, the young Danish immigrant was in despair. All his dreams of going back to Ribe either as a rich man or as a gallant soldier were gone, and with them all reasonable hope of winning Elisabeth for his bride. Yet because he loved her so much he still thought of her constantly and, in spite of everything, somehow believed that one day she must be his wife.

2

From
One Thing
to Another

> "All things come to those who
> wait—and fight for them."
> —*The Making of an American*

Once again Jacob Riis found himself in New Jersey. It
took him four days to get to Camden, the town across the
river from Philadelphia. He lived mostly on apples he
picked up under old trees. Nights were too cold to spend
in the fields, so he slept in lonely barns. The last few miles
he rode in a cattle car and the good-hearted police captain
on duty in the Camden freight yards let him sleep in an
empty cell. The next morning the kind man insisted on
giving Jacob his breakfast, money to get his shoes
blacked, and his ferry fare to Philadelphia.

Pocketing his pride, Jacob went to the Danish consul
there. The consul and his wife proved to be good friends.
They kept their countryman with them for two weeks,
fattening him up a bit and putting him in a more cheerful
frame of mind. Then they sent him to Jamestown, New
York, where there was a colony of Scandinavians, among
them an old schoolmate of Jacob's. Through the cold
northern winter—his first in America—Jacob lived with a

Danish family, working first at making cradles in a furniture shop and then outside, felling trees and cutting ice on the nearby lake.

After his rugged experiences and his many months alone, Jacob enjoyed the companionship of the Danes and Swedes. He went to weekly parties in Jamestown wearing a coat he had bought for a dollar in a Philadelphia secondhand shop. His Danish roommate had no such formal attire, so Jacob let him wear the coat every other week. Twice a week he attended a Scandinavian society's evening meetings and, because most of the members were less well informed than he was and because he enjoyed talking, Jacob offered to give a course of lectures on astronomy and geology. All went well until one evening he got mixed up trying to explain longitude and latitude. An old sea captain set him straight, but the audience lost confidence in its young lecturer and one by one walked out on him, ending the lecture course. Later on, when Riis had to deal with statistics and had trouble with them, he admitted he never did have a head for mathematics!

In the early spring Jacob hunted and trapped muskrats; but as full spring arrived, he had the urge to move on. He was as determined as ever to become a success and go back to Denmark and marry Elisabeth, and this kind of life, he realized, would not help that dream come true. He carefully paid every cent he owed, then set out to walk to Buffalo. Never one to save, he started out with very little cash in his pocket.

On the way to Buffalo, Riis worked at various jobs. He spent a month with a doctor and his family as their hired man, also helping one of the young sons with his studies and teaching him some fencing tricks. The doctor urged

Jacob to stay on, but being a hired man was not his idea
of a successful career, so he went on to Buffalo. There he
worked in a lumberyard, in a planing mill, a cabinet-
maker's, with a railroad gang, and in the shipyards. Always there was some reason for his leaving one job for another—poor pay, a quarrel, the job's coming to an end,
or his being discharged for being "too blamed independent."

Evenings Riis spent reading and practicing the writing
of English. He tried his hand at writing essays, usually
about the German mistreatment of the Danes, about
which he felt so strongly, but he never ventured to send
his efforts to a publisher. He wanted to gain more fluency
with English, to be able to make his words "pour." After
much thought he had decided on what he wanted to be.
He would become a newspaper reporter, and for this the
mastery of words, he knew, was important.

Riis's ambition was not as strange as it might seem. In
Denmark he had helped his father edit the small-town
weekly paper—a job that supplemented the teacher's
salary, so inadequate to support a large family. Jacob had
enjoyed this newspaper work. Reporting, he decided, was
"the highest and noblest of all callings"; it would be both
an interesting and an important profession. He did not
doubt his ability to be a good reporter. He liked meeting
people and he liked working with words.

Sure now of his purpose in life, Riis went to a Buffalo
newspaper office and applied for a job as a reporter. It did
not bother him that his hands were rough from shipyard
work or that he looked like what he was—a foreign-born
laborer. But it infuriated him to have the man who inter-
viewed him laugh at his ambition and then rudely dismiss

him, shutting the door in his face. Jacob reopened it and shouted angrily, "You laugh now, but wait—" Slamming the door after him, Jacob Riis vowed at that moment that, come what might, nothing or no one would stop him from becoming a reporter.

Just then, however, an opportunity came to him that made him put aside for the time being his newspaper ambition. Some of his Scandinavian friends in Jamestown invited him to join them in a cooperative furniture-making factory they were starting. Here was a chance to get rich fast! Oil had been discovered in western Pennsylvania; people were flocking into the region; they had money and they needed furniture. Riis's job would be to sell it to them.

And so Jacob Riis became a furniture salesman. He studied the album of photographs of the pieces of furniture to be sold, then started out. From the beginning he had amazing success in getting orders. This pleased him, although he did not understand why practically all the orders were for only one item—an extension table. Why was it that everyone seemed to want this and nothing else? Alas, the reason was that the price listed for the table was wrong—so low, in fact, that it was less than the cost of making it.

The young firm, discovering the mistake, tried to get in touch with their salesman to call him back. But Jacob, hopping from place to place happily gathering orders, could not be reached for several days. When he finally received the urgent message to return, he decided that, since business was so good, he would just fill up his order book before turning back. In the Jamestown factory at last, Jacob learned the sad truth. Instead of his orders helping, they—added to the price error—had plunged the firm into bankruptcy. The orders were canceled, with difficulty, and Riis's commission, which he had figured in hundreds of dollars, was exactly zero.

Riis did not blame anyone. But now, believing himself to be a supersalesman, he spent his last seventy-five cents for a sample of a fluting iron for which the New York manufacturers needed a traveling salesman. When the sample iron arrived, Riis took the precaution of having a friend try it out to make sure it could both iron skirts and "flute the flounces," as promised. It could, so he set out to sell fluting irons, first in Jamestown and then in Pittsburgh. Everything again looked rosy.

One day as Jacob passed a horse market, he saw a fine young horse being auctioned off. Someone had just bid eighteen dollars. On the spur of the moment, thinking how wonderful it would be to own a horse and ride out into the country, Riis raised the bid to nineteen and got the horse. This left him with only six dollars in his pocket, and as he led the animal away he began to think of the difficulties ahead. First of all, he couldn't ride. Even if he were able to, he couldn't very well take orders for fluting irons while riding around on a horse. Worst of all, how in the world could he afford to feed both the horse and himself? He sat down on the curb to think things over. When, at that moment, the man who had bid the eighteen dollars came along, Riis stopped him, explained matters, and agreed to sell the horse to him at the eighteen-dollar figure. At least, he figured, he had owned a horse, if only for a few moments. He would try to believe this was a satisfaction worth the dollar it had cost him.

14

For a while the fluting-iron business went well. Jacob even traveled as far west as Chicago in the belief that there were great prospects ahead. Then the bottom fell out of everything. The company he was working for misled and defrauded him, and acquaintances to whom he had loaned money ran away with it. He returned to western Pennsylvania where, in a lonely inn, he fell ill with a fever. As he lay there bad matters became worse: he learned in a letter from his family that finally reached him that his Elisabeth was betrothed to a dashing Danish soldier.

Now nothing seemed to matter. He had a relapse and for a while lay ill and hopeless. But being young and by nature optimistic, he recovered and set out again, though sadly, heading east. The life of a traveling salesman no longer appealed to him, and for the moment he had lost sight of his goal of becoming a newspaperman. Still lovesick, he decided to learn the new skill of telegraphy and in some remote place live out a solitary existence as a telegraph operator. In New York he invested his last twenty dollars in a telegraphy course. He found he could attend classes in the afternoon, so he spent his mornings trying to support himself by peddling irons from house to house.

A newspaper ad for a city editor on a Long Island weekly political paper brought to life Jacob's deepseated ambition. He applied for the job, got it without trouble, and for two weeks busied himself gathering and writing up local news in the Long Island community. But as there was no sign of pay for his work and every day more indication of the paper's going bankrupt, he left. Back in Manhattan he returned to house-to-house selling.

Instead of peddling irons, he now sold—or tried to sell—a book by Charles Dickens, appropriately entitled *Hard Times.*

Three wasted years, Jacob thought as, at the end of a discouraging day, he sat on a doorstep. Beside him crouched an affectionate Newfoundland puppy someone had given him and that he could not bring himself to part with, in spite of the feeding and lodging problems. The dog growled as a passerby stopped in front of them, but Jacob was so wrapped up in his worries that he scarcely looked up. When he did, he saw it was the principal of the telegraphy school he had attended. After a friendly greeting, the principal, who knew of his former pupil's interest in newspaper work, spoke of an opening he had heard about on Newspaper Row. Jacob's eyes brightened. The principal suggested they go to his office, which was nearby, and there he would write a note of introduction. Jacob gladly accepted his offer. The note written, the principal turned his attention to the Newfoundland puppy, to which he had taken a great fancy. He offered to adopt him and give him a good home. For the sake of the dog, Jacob agreed, although he was sorry to lose the friendly pup.

The next morning, in better spirits, with his newspaper ambition revived and the prospect of a job as cub reporter, Jacob hurried to Park Row. When he presented the note of introduction at the New York News Association office, he was looked at rather doubtfully. But he was given a trial assignment—to cover a special luncheon at the opulent Astor House Hotel. Faint with hunger, young Riis almost swooned at the sight and smell of food he could not taste, but he managed to turn in a satisfactory report and to get the job—at ten dollars a week.

Almost delirious with hunger and joy, he headed for the modest Danish boardinghouse where he could now promise to pay his way. On its steps he collapsed, and there he lay until someone arrived and helped him up the stairs. Food and rest soon restored him, and he began to dream again of a bright future. Now that his foot was set on the first rung of the newspaper-world ladder, Jacob resolved he "would reach the top or die climbing."

3
Romantic Journey

> "It is true that all the world loves a
> lover. It smiled on me all day long,
> and I smiled back."
>
> —*The Making of an American*

Jacob Riis was once more filled with hope. He would not
let his mind dwell on the thought that the girl he loved
was engaged to another. At least, as far as he knew, she
was not married. He did not blame her family, the richest
and most important in Ribe, for opposing the marriage of
their lovely daughter to an ordinary carpenter. But if he
could become a successful American newspaperman,
surely that would be a different matter. Then they might
withdraw their opposition; they might even favor the
match. And he was certain he could make Elisabeth see
that he and she were meant for each other.

Jacob put everything he had into his work. He was
surprised at the way all the things he knew and had
picked up in his three years in America came in handy.
"There is scarcely anything one can learn that will not
sooner or later be useful to a newspaperman," he said
later. His written English was still far from perfect, but
the color and enthusiasm of his reports more than over-
balanced this lack. The New York News Association
never had a more willing or harder-working employee.
Luckily he was a great walker, for there were as yet no
electric cars or elevated railroads to ride to distant loca-

tions, the straw-carpeted horsecars were slow and cold, and cabs were expensive. All reports had to be taken into the office in person, for there were few telephones available to call them in. Since the News Association sold items to both morning and evening papers, the working day began at ten in the morning and often did not end until long after midnight. If there happened to be a free hour during the day, Jacob filled it with reading or practicing his telegraphy.

After a few months of this strenuous life, he was offered a job as reporter on a small weekly newspaper in Brooklyn. The pay was better—fifteen dollars a week—and it looked like a good opportunity to get ahead. The four-page paper was run to promote the interests of a political party. The new reporter was to supply items that would attract readers, who would then go on to read the political propaganda provided by the paper's owners.

Riis worked at his customary furious pace, giving such satisfaction to his employers that they soon gave him the title of editor, a ten-dollar-a-week raise—and more work. With the raise he started his first bank account. But that fall of 1874 the owners found themselves in debt and, the election over, they had little reason for going on with the paper. They instructed Riis to sell the type to the foundry for whatever it would bring. Tired and discouraged, he did not much care that this would mean the end of his job as editor. Christmas was near and he was alone, far from his family and friends, and with his sweetheart pledged to marry someone else.

On Christmas Eve came a letter from his family that changed everything. It told of the death of his two older brothers from tuberculosis, the dread disease then called consumption. And in a postscript, as if it were of little interest, it mentioned the death of Elisabeth's soldier fiancé. Swept by conflicting emotions, Riis lay on his bed and wept. Then he went out to find the paper's owners. Using all his powers of persuasion, he got them to agree to sell him their little paper for six hundred and fifty dollars. He would give them the seventy-five dollars he had saved as down payment and sign notes for the balance. Considering their debts and the comparatively small amount they would get for their type, and knowing Riis's ability and energy, the owners figured this might not be a bad deal.

A period of frenzied activity followed, as Riis, single-handed, ran the *South Brooklyn News*. He gathered the news items, wrote the copy, solicited the ads, brought the sheets, still damp from the press, from the printer's in Manhattan to the small office in South Brooklyn, and hired newsboys to hawk the papers on the street.

To the delight of both the old owners and the new one, the venture was tremendously successful. In six months' time Riis was able to pay off the last of the notes. Then, and not till then, did he write his beloved Elisabeth. It was his first letter to her since the note of good wishes he had painfully written after he had learned of her engagement to the Danish soldier. He spent the better part of a night composing his offer of marriage and in the morning carried the letter to the post office to see it safely started on its way.

Weeks went by without a reply. In uncertainty, yet with his usual optimism, Riis went on with his day-and-night push to continue the success of his paper. He wanted to have more, much more, to offer Elisabeth.

20

Every day he looked for a letter from her. At last it came. Fortunately it was not the one she had written just after receiving his proposal; that, which had been a refusal, he never did receive. This second letter was written after months of thoughtful reconsideration and pondering over the advice of her dying fiancé that if, after his death, a good man who loved her asked her to be his wife, she should accept. She realized, as she wrote later, "that he [Jacob] was just as faithful as ever to his idea that we were meant for one another, and that [though] 'I might say him No time and time again, the day would come when I would change my mind.' "

Jacob, hesitating in dread to read the letter, finally tore open the envelope. When he read its contents he learned that Elisabeth had been teaching in a small town; that she was lonely; that she appreciated his faithfulness to her and valued his love; and that, if he still wished it and would come for her after a while, she would become his wife and return with him to live in America.

In his excitement and joy, Riis paced the floor of his little room until at last his landlord came up to see what was wrong. Learning the glad news, he stayed to hear more about Elisabeth and to wish his lodger happiness.

In the next weeks Riis went through the motions of his daily work wrapped in clouds of joy. He wrote Elisabeth that in a few months, when he had a little more to offer her, he would return to Denmark to make her his bride. But he was an impatient man, far too impatient to wait long enough to put aside a really adequate nest egg for married life. When he had a chance to sell his paper for five times what he had paid for it, he let it go and sailed for Europe.

At Hamburg, where his ship landed, Jacob was in such a mad rush to get to Ribe that he got aboard the wrong train and had to spend the night in an unknown little town. The next day, on the right train at last, he counted the minutes till he would reach Ribe. After a station stop a few miles from there, the door of his compartment opened and who should enter but his father and his father's friend, the family doctor! They had been visiting a friend in the nearby town. Jacob's father, looking as if he must be seeing a ghost, steadied himself against the door. Then there was a joyous reunion. Another followed when they reached the Riis home and the boy from America was greeted by his mother, younger brothers and sister, and his foster sister, Emma.

After a happy meal together, dimmed only by the memory of the deaths of the oldest sons, Jacob excused himself to go out on an unannounced errand. Would he not take a younger brother with him? his parents asked. But Jacob insisted on going alone.

He crossed the Long Bridge over the Nibs River and climbed the little hill crowned by the largest house in town, often called the Castle. It was New Year's Day and he knew Elisabeth was spending the holidays with her family. A maid answered his knock and ushered him into the same little room where, almost six years before, he had proposed marriage to Elisabeth and had been rejected. He remembered well how he had stumbled from the room, his eyes wet with tears. But he had refused to accept defeat; he had held steadfastly to his dream, and now he was here again—but with such a difference!

Elisabeth appeared, interrupting his reverie. In his eyes she was even lovelier than she had been at sixteen. He looked at her adoringly, and distance, time, and misunderstandings melted away as if by magic.

Hours later he returned to his own home and in an unsteady voice said to his parents, "I came home to give you Elisabeth for a daughter. She has promised to be my wife."

His mother wept. His father opened the Bible before him and read, "Unto Thy name give glory, O Lord."

There followed a few weeks of courtship during which Elisabeth learned to think of Jacob as more than just an annoyingly persistant suitor, and her parents dropped their objection to the marriage. Jacob's family had always loved Elisabeth. The whole town, always interested in a local romance, took especial delight in this unexpected match.

Jacob and Elisabeth were married in March, 1876, in the centuries-old Ribe Domkirke. Loving friends brought flowers for the bride to wear—flowers they had "grown in winter-gardens in the scant sunlight of the long Northern winter—'loved-up' they say." And then, as relatives and friends waved good-by, the young couple entered the mail-coach drawn by a pair of horses and set out on their long journey to America.

"I knew in my soul that I should conquer," Riis wrote years later. "For her head was leaning trustfully on my shoulder and her hand was in mine; and all was well."

Elisabeth, quiet, lovely, poised, was a perfect counterpart to Jacob's more impulsive nature. She was a homebody and did her best to make the little flat Jacob found for them in South Brooklyn a real home. But though she tried, she could not altogether conceal her longing for the Old Country. Jacob did his best to help her overcome her homesickness, sometimes pretending not to notice, sometimes putting on an apron and helping with the unaccustomed cooking. He was very happy. He had the wife of his dreams; they were "comrades for better or worse from the day she put her hand in mine, and never was there a more loyal and faithful one."

Riis had agreed when he sold his paper that he would not start another in the same area for ten years. By now his savings were pretty well exhausted, but with Elisabeth beside him this did not bother him too much. "Two, we would beat the world," he declared. He felt confident he could turn up something to tide them over until he found what he really wanted—a reporter's job on a New York daily newspaper.

Always intrigued by something new, without being too concerned over its intricacies, Riis bought a stereopticon outfit—a "magic lantern"—and put it in the basement. It was run by a gas contrivance that two friends volunteered to help set up. They tried to follow directions, but they nearly blew up the house before they finally mastered the technique.

An ingenious idea had occurred to Riis. Why not use the stereopticon as an advertising device? Brooklyn stores sold their merchandise to people living farther out on Long Island. Riis called on store managers and talked several of them into letting him put on an outdoor show in communities where they wanted to attract customers. He alternated store ads with interesting color views from his own collection. The scheme worked so well that it was extended to more places and went on for the entire fall season. When cold weather arrived, Riis set up his apparatus in a downtown Brooklyn window. The next

24

summer he and a friend took the stereopticon equipment to upstate New York where they planned to start an elaborate promotional program. But a railroad strike and labor violence interfered, forcing them to give up their idea.

For some time Riis had been trying to find a place for himself as a reporter on one of the New York papers, but without success. Several times he had approached Mr. Shanks, the city editor of the *New York Tribune,* who lived in South Brooklyn not far from the young Riises. At first the answer had been negative; then it became merely evasive. Finally Mr. Shanks agreed to give the energetic young man a chance.

The *Tribune* was known as a great newspaper, and Jacob Riis was delighted to become connected with it. As he assured Mr. Shanks, his own standards were high and he would not do anything to lessen the *Tribune*'s fine reputation. His reporting would first of all be accurate. "The power of fact," he wrote later, "is the mightiest lever of this or of any day. The reporter has his hand upon it, and it is his grievious fault if he does not use it well."

In an age before radio or television, people relied on newspapers to tell them what was going on in the city, the nation, and the world. Riis believed a good reporter had a responsibility to "sift wrong from right." This he intended to do. Now that he had the break he had been looking for, he determined to be not just a good reporter but one of the best.

4

Police Reporter
on
Mulberry Street

> "The reporter who is behind the
> scenes sees the tumult of passions
> and not rarely a human heroism
> that redeems all the rest."
>
> —*The Making of an American*

For several months Riis rushed all over the city in his job
as general reporter for the *New York Tribune*. He was
on trial, the work was hard, and the pay was small, but he
gloried in being a newspaper reporter, especially on the
influential *Tribune*. Every week he could feel his work
growing better. Mr. Shanks, he thought, must notice this
too.

One winter day, rushing to "catch the edition," Riis
ran full tilt into two men coming out of the side door of
the *Tribune* building. The impact was so great that it
knocked one of them off his feet and into a nearby snow-
drift. Riis realized with horror that the man he had
knocked down was Mr. Shanks. Apologies seemed useless.
Speechless, he recovered his editor's snow-covered hat
and held it out to him.

"Do you always run like that when you are out on
assignments?" Mr. Shanks asked angrily.

"When it is late like this, yes," Riis answered, recovering his voice. "How else would I get my copy in?"

Mr. Shanks brushed the snow from his coat. "Well, just take a reef in when you come round the corner," he advised.

The next day Riis was summoned to the city editor's desk. He fully expected to be fired. Instead, Mr. Shanks remarked that he had worked out a way to prevent being knocked down again. "Our man at Police Headquarters has left," he said. "I am going to send you up there in his place. You can run there all you want to, and you will want to all you can. It is a place that needs a man who will run to get his copy in and tell the truth and stick to it. You will find plenty of fighting there. But don't go knocking people down—unless you have to."

Riis could hardly believe his ears. He knew police reporting was a hard assignment and he was a bit afraid of it. He had heard, too, that at the Mulberry Street office rivalry with reporters from other papers was keen. But he was reassured by the confidence Mr. Shanks showed in him and pleased with the increase in salary he was given. He telegraphed his young wife to tell her the news, then cleared his desk and set out for Mulberry Street. He had only a vague notion of what his new job would mean, but he soon learned that a police reporter was "the man who gathers and handles all the news that means trouble to some one; the murders, fires, suicides, robberies, and all that sort, before it gets into court." Given a choice, this was not the kind of reporting he would have picked, but he resolved he would make good at the new job.

On Mulberry Street, Jacob Riis had need of every bit of his fighting spirit. Reporters from rival papers also on night duty were housed in the same building, directly across from the city Police Headquarters. The rumors about competition were all too true. The other reporters immediately banded together to "finish off the Dutchman," as they called the *Tribune*'s new man. At first, by playing all sorts of lowdown tricks on him, they almost succeeded. After a week the manager of the Associated Press Bureau, which the *Tribune* represented, told Mr. Shanks he did not think the new man on Mulberry Street would do. "Wait and see," Mr. Shanks was reported to have replied.

"They stole my slips in the telegraph office and substituted others that sent me off on a wild-goose chase to the farthest river wards in the midnight hour, thinking so to tire me out. But they did it once too often. I happened on a very important case on such a trip, and made the most of it," Riis wrote later.

After that incident, the Mulberry Street police reporters settled down to a long-drawn-out contest of wits. "I hit as hard as I knew how," Riis admitted, "and so did they." Although Riis claimed he had no detective skill, he was able to fit the various pieces of a skimpy police report together like a jigsaw puzzle and he had the persistence to play every angle of every lead for all it was worth. One distinct advantage over his rivals was that the *Tribune* had the only telegraph wire in the building and he knew how to use it.

All the police newspaper reporters got their leads from the precinct reports posted in Police Headquarters. They also had access to the nearby Health Department's daily files. In addition, all of them tried to get "inside stories" by cultivating friendships with key officials and others in the district.

Riis's method was to make a selection of the police-blotter items he considered of greatest importance or interest, think them over carefully, then do the necessary follow-through legwork. For this he had as a partner the loyal and capable Amos Ensign. Crime reporting, the tenderhearted Riis found both physically and emotionally exhausting. It depressed him to visit sordid scenes of tragedy and violence. Try as he would, he could not be impersonal about them. Here, he felt, were great human dramas, and he tried to grasp the motives that lay behind the acts. He continued to be "a reporter of facts," but in addition he tried to "catch the human drift" in his stories. If at all possible, he wanted to tell his readers not only *what* had happened but *why* it had happened as it had, and to make them feel its pathos, shock, or thrill.

Lincoln Steffens was a young journalist who was sent to Mulberry Street to investigate rumors of police corruption. Jacob Riis took him in hand and showed him the way around in what Steffens called "a dark mysterious layer of the life of a great city." The budding journalist was impressed by the difference between the usual crime reports and Riis's. Most police reporters, he said, wrote up their items as news; Riis wrote them up "as stories, with heart, humor, and understanding." Steffens sometimes considered Riis's reactions to unhappy situations oversensitive, and his outbursts when he learned of some nasty bit of corruption overviolent, but he had great respect for Riis's ability and for his staunch character. He was, said Steffens, "such a good man to know," with "emotion to suffer and a kind, fighting spirit to weep, whoop, laugh, and demand."

The year Riis went to Mulberry Street a gruesome grave robbery made news of the sensational sort many New Yorkers relished reading. Some of Riis's rival reporters continued to keep tension high by inventing a story of a soon-expected breakthrough that would solve the crime. Their papers sold wildly as people looked for the promised news. Riis spent hours sifting every scrap of evidence. Convinced that his opponents' statements were a hoax, he courageously maintained this point of view in his stories. The *Tribune* let him do this; it also let him know that if he missed out on a big break, his days with the paper would be over. Things grew so tense that Mr. Shanks left his desk and went to Mulberry Street to work on the case with Riis and Ensign.

At last the bubble burst and the story of the promised breakthrough was proven to be entirely fictitious. The guilty reporters were fined or suspended by their papers. The *Tribune* gave Riis a raise, and Mr. Shanks issued a bulletin stating: "By zeal, activity and faithful recognition of the *Tribune* rule of exchanging news with no other paper Mr. Riis has done much to make the *Tribune* police reports the best in the city." These words of praise from his editor meant more to Riis than the raise, much as he needed the money.

Riis's loyalty to his paper and his high standards of duty were appreciated at the *Tribune* by more than the city editor. Once Riis was suspended for something not his fault and that, being angry, he refused to explain. That night a big fire broke out in the downtown warehouse district. From his Brooklyn home, Riis could see the smoke and flames. He could not stand not being on the spot to see and report the disaster, and finally he hurried to the scene and observed it all. Then he went to the *Tribune* office to write up his report. Temporarily without a desk because of his suspension, he had to ask for one. The night editor, who knew that, being suspended, Riis had no obligation to cover the fire, got up from his desk, held out his hand, and said, "Take mine." The next day the suspension order was lifted.

The whole area around Police Headquarters was known as Mulberry Bend because the street there, in Riis's words, "crooks like an elbow." This district was acknowledged to be the worst in the city, with the largest number of crimes and acts of violence. Following up police items led Riis night after night into its dark, filthy alleys and airless, overcrowded tenements. In a single night he might cover a tenement-house fire, a murder, a robbery, and a gun battle between cops and a lawless gang.

Riis had no fear of poking around in the Bend in the middle of the night. "No man, sober, minding his own business, and wearing a quiet air of authority and acting as if he had a right to be where he is, runs much risk in the slums," he said confidently. Perhaps because he wore a slouch hat and, on account of nearsightedness, spectacles, Riis was often taken for a physician and addressed as "Doc." This added to his safety for, as he explained, "Doctors are never molested in the slum. It does not know but that its turn to need them is coming next." More than once "Doc" was a witness to a stabbing or shooting and was called on to help the ambulance doctors.

It was Riis's natural interest in people that made him

look beneath the surface of the stories he covered. He could not forget that most of the persons involved had come, as he had, from a European country, expecting to find America "a land of opportunity." He could see how they had become disillusioned as they struggled for survival under intolerable conditions. He remembered how this had happened to him, too, for a time, when he was a ragged, penniless immigrant on these very streets. He too had been so downcast and depressed that at times he had almost lost the will to live and this in spite of having advantages most of these people did not have. He had known the English language and had possessed a skill. Most of these slum-dwellers were ignorant and unskilled. They were forced to live crowded together in buildings unfit for human beings and they did not know how to fight effectively against the injustices imposed on them.

Riis's sense of outrage at this situation deepened with time and experience. More and more often he could not resist writing into his stories a plea to give these people of the slums a fairer chance in life.

"Give the facts, sparing comments," his editor advised him. But he could not; the facts touched him too deeply. In spite of warnings he continued to write in his own way, tinging his vigorous, sensitive stories with his own convictions. Yet he was not fired; he had become too good a reporter for the paper to lose. "In the end the complaints died out," Riis said. "I suppose I was given up as hopeless." But perhaps the real truth was that the *Tribune* editors realized the importance of what Lincoln Steffens had said: "Riis was a reporter who not only got the news; he cared about the news." And he did his best to make others care, too!

5

"Mulberry Bend Must Go!"

> "When a thing is right, it is bound
> to come, if we make it come."
> —*Charities*, September 15, 1903

Jacob Riis was not the first to raise his voice against conditions in the New York slums. As early as 1844 a city inspector, Dr. Griscom, stated in a report: "We are parties to their [the slum-dwellers'] degradation inasmuch as we permit the inhabitation of places, from which it is not possible improvements in condition or habits can come. We suffer the sublandlords to stow them, like cattle, in pens and to compel them to swallow poison with every breath. They are allowed, may it not be said required, to live in dirt."

But the doctor's words had little effect. Corrupt politicians and greedy landlords saw a chance to line their pockets at the expense of the slum-dwellers, and the "good" people, the "comfortably fixed" people, were indifferent. They took poverty for granted. It had always existed; it would go on existing. Overcrowding, drunkenness, disease, disorder, and crime just naturally went along with poverty, they thought. The reason the poor were as they were, many "good" people said—and some of them really believed—was because they were shiftless, afraid of

33

work, and preferred to be dirty. These "good" people helped to make up the traditional Christmas baskets for the needy in the community, but on the whole found it simpler to contribute to missions in Africa than to try to relieve the suffering of the poor close at hand.

But when their convenience was affected or their safety endangered, the public could become aroused into taking action. This happened during the cholera epidemic of the 1850's. When the terrible disease was rampant in the overcrowded slum section and threatened to spread throughout the city, a frightened citizenry insisted that New York authorities tear down the worst neighborhood, the notorious Five Points (also known as Murderers' Alley and Den of Thieves). The state legislature took action too, passing long overdue sanitary laws affecting tenement houses. One of these laws required an "annual inspection of privies."

In the years following the Civil War, New York became the center of the garment trade and of cigar-making and other industries, and employers looked for cheap labor. They welcomed laborers from inland America and from across the Atlantic without giving much thought to where the newcomers could live. The immigrants who flocked in from oppressed countries in Europe, hoping to find a better life in America, naturally wanted to live close to possible work and to earlier immigrants who spoke their language.

Lower Manhattan, where industries were concentrated, became badly overcrowded. The well-to-do residents of this oldest part of the city had moved farther north, and their spacious old homes offered a tempting opportunity to smart businessmen. Property owners and their agents

34

discovered they could rent practically anything to new-comers for a high price, payable in advance. They cut up the old houses into flats with closet-sized, often window-less rooms. Behind these remodeled homes, in the spaces where gardens had been, they put up five- and six-story buildings into which they crammed as many people as humanly (or inhumanly) possible. No matter that the tiny rooms were dark, airless, waterless firetraps, cold in winter and unbearably hot in summer; greedy landlords were able to rent them at outrageous prices. They even subdivided and rented the old stables that had been on the estates, as well as leaky garrets of old houses and damp, rat-infested cellars. Such places quickly deteriorated into slums and became hangouts for criminals as well as the living quarters of the very poorest of the European im-migrants.

Riis described Mulberry Bend as "ordinary enough to look at from the street, but pierced by a maze of foul alleys, in the depths of which skulked the tramp and the outcast thief with loathsome wrecks that had once laid claim to the name of woman. Every foot of it reeked with incest and murder. Bandits' Roost, Bottle Alley, were names synonymous with robbery and redhanded outrage. By night, in its worst days, I have gone poking about the shuddering haunts with a policeman on the beat and come away in a ferment of anger and disgust that would keep me awake far into the morning hours planning means of its destruction."

Mulberry Bend was, said Riis, "the wickedest, as it was the foulest, spot in the city. . . . It was not fit for pigs to be in, let alone human beings." Nothing short of its com-plete demolition would satisfy him. "To me," he confessed, "the whole battle with the slum had summed itself up in the struggle with this dark spot." To explain this, he referred to his own early immigrant days. "If I made it [Mulberry Bend] my own concern to the exclusion of all else, it was only because I knew it. I had been part of it. Homeless and alone I had sought its shelter, not for long—that was not to be endured—but long enough to taste its poison, and I hated it. I knew the blow must be struck there, to kill."

To see innocent people, especially women and children, forced to live in such a place was almost more than Riis could endure. Often, as he returned to his office after a trip to one of its "dens of death," Riis would shake his fist and mutter, "Mulberry Bend must go!" Becoming known as the "Mulberry Bend crank" did not bother him; what did bother him was that not many others seemed to share his concern.

Often it was broad daylight before Riis reached home after his night's work. When he had written up his newspaper stories, he would walk down Mulberry Street to the Fulton Street ferry, which took him across the East River to Brooklyn. He preferred walking to taking the horsecars on the nearby Bowery. In this way, he said, "I saw the slum when off its guard."

This was something to see, especially during the summer months. Then, Riis wrote, "Half the tenement population sleep out of doors, in streets and yards, on the roof, or on the fire escape." For in New York's summer heat, he said, "Even a truck in the street or a crowded fire escape becomes a bedroom infinitely preferable to any the house affords." Despite "summer doctors," sent into the district by the Board of Health, the summer months were the "death season" for children and babies.

The tenement house was, Riis believed, the heart of the slum problem. "In one way or another," he wrote, "it is found directly responsible for, or intimately associated with, three-fourths of the misery of the poor." How was a happy home life possible when a father, mother, and their children, with perhaps a lodger or two to help them pay the rent, had to live in one or two tiny, sunless, smelly rooms, unbearably hot in summer and often freezingly cold in winter? In many tenements water had to be carried, sometimes up four or five flights, from the squealing pumps in the outside court. Occasionally, when water was most needed, the pumps would run dry. In one block of rear tenements there were five hundred babies and not a single bathtub. It was in these rear tenements that the death rate was highest. Here one out of every five babies died and one year (1888) one out of every three.

Although Riis came to know this district well, he could still lose his way among the rear houses "set at all sorts of angles, with odd, winding passages or no passages at all, only 'runways' for the thieves and toughs of the neighborhood."

One of these alleys—Cat Alley—Riis called "my alley. It was mine by right of long acquaintance. We were neighbors for twenty years." It was not really an alley, he explained, but "a row of four or five old tenements in a back yard that was reached by a passageway somewhat less than three feet wide between the sheer walls of the front houses." Its occupants were a mixture of Irish, German, French, Jewish, and Italian families. The women frequently "scrapped," but still there was a human fellowship, a "rude sense of justice," and when anyone was in need, the others were quick to help. The sun never reached most of these buildings. Yet it was not unusual for the tenants to pay the landlord half of their combined family earnings, leaving them next to nothing for food and clothing.

Often, when Riis entered a tenement-house hall, he could hear "doors opening softly on every landing as the strange step is heard on the stairs." Tenants lived in fear of the collector arriving to demand the rent, or insurance money, or some other payment. They had so little money that, Riis declared, "I am satisfied from my own observation that hundreds of men, women, and children are every day slowly starving to death in the tenements."

Some of the tenement cellars held cruller bakeries, which operated at night. The deep fat in which the crullers were boiled sometimes spilled over into the fire, making flames blaze up. If the fire shot up through the old timbers, it cut off all possibility of escape for the tenants sleeping on the floors above. "A fire in the night in one of those human beehives, with its terror and woe, is one of the things that live in the recollection ever after as a terrible nightmare," Riis wrote, adding, "I suppose that I had to do with a hundred such fires as a police reporter." He quoted the testimony of the chief of the Fire Department at a hearing after one "cruller fire": "Tenements are erected mainly with a view of returning a large income for the amount of capital invested. It is only after a fire in which great loss of life occurs that any interest whatever is taken in the safety of its occupants."

Riis was so stirred by the sights he saw in Mulberry Bend, both while on duty and during his night walks to the ferry, that he said, "I felt that I must tell of them, or burst." If he could only transfer to his readers the picture he had of the Bend, he was certain "the community would help settle with that pigsty according to its deserts."

And so he continued to introduce into his newspaper stories more and more about the foulness of the slum and the exploitation of the poor by greedy landlords and heartless employers. He wrote touchingly of the slum-dwellers' despair at heartbreaking disappointments, when they were unable to get work or when disaster struck. He told of their inability to cope with their living and working conditions. He showed the need for stricter enforcement of the few regulations that did exist and for new tenement-house-control laws. He urged his readers to work for these reforms, but little happened. Riis's innate faith in the goodness of people and in the power of the press was sorely tested, and he wrote wearily, "It takes a lot of telling to make a city know when it is doing wrong."

A year of night duty on Mulberry Street brought Jacob Riis to the point where he was so emotionally over-wrought that he felt he could not go on, and he asked for a transfer back to general reporting. His request was refused. Mr. Shanks and others at the *Tribune* were beginning to realize the importance of this man.

"Go back and stay," Mr. Shanks told him. "Unless I am much mistaken, you are finding something up there that needs you."

"And so," said Riis, "I was turned back to the task I wanted to shirk." But the strain was eased by his being shifted from night to day duty.

The war with the rival reporters continued. Riis discovered that they usually did not appear at their offices until around noon, so he made a point of arriving at eleven. This forced them to do the same or run the risk of letting the *Tribune* scoop them on some important story. When Riis saw the others getting in at eleven, he advanced his arrival time to nine. Highly annoyed, they followed suit. Then Riis started getting to his office at eight, and morning work began to be commonplace all over the reporters' Mulberry Street building.

Never afraid of hard work, Riis pushed himself unmercifully. He tried to report everything both accurately and in depth. Completely confident now of his writing ability, he was convinced his mission in life was to use it to awaken an indifferent public to the desperate situation of the poor people in their city. He acknowledged that this awakening process was slow. "People do not like to have their rest disturbed," he observed. "I wrote, but it seemed to make no impression."

Then came the miracle of the flash light. When Riis read a brief account of its invention in Europe, he became very excited. Here was just what he needed! No one could argue with the evidence presented by a photograph, and a flash light would make it possible to catch the evils of the slum at night, when things were even worse than in the day. By showing families trying to sleep crowded into tiny rooms, by exposing the sordid night life of the saloons, by picturing tramps sleeping in "five-cent spots" and children huddled in cellar doorways, he might perhaps prod the public into taking action.

So, in 1887, Jacob Riis became America's first documentary reporter-photographer. Already an amateur cameraman, he began experimenting with the new invention. Taking with him a few friends interested in photography, he invaded a slum tenement at night, armed with a camera and with the pistol that contained the cartridges filled with the flash-light powder. But when he fired it, the terrified tenants "bolted through windows and down fire-escapes." The next time Riis substituted a frying pan for the pistol, flashing the light on the pan. This was more successful, though twice he set the room on fire and once himself, and only the fact that he wore glasses saved his eyes.

Riis's friends soon lost interest in giving up their sleep for night excursions into the slum, so he hired a professional photographer to go with him and take the pictures. When this man tried to sell the photographs behind Riis's back and pocket the money, Riis decided the only thing to do was to work by himself. He kept on experimenting until, in spite of his impatience and his clumsiness with mechanical devices, he was able to produce remarkably effective photographs.

The success of Jacob Riis's photographs lay not only in their technique but in their detail and emphasis on the human factor. Each picture told a story, often grim, often dramatic, often moving. Each portrayed a definite feature of slum life—an overcrowded room where a large family lived and worked, a dirty narrow alley, a stale-beer dive, a filthy police lodging-room, a dismal jail cell. The Riis photographs came to be shown in courts as evidence, and they canceled out many claims of City Hall, many statements of landlords and politicians, many pleas of "sweatshop" tenants. They brought about such a change in court evidence that it has been said that, after Riis, "the facts became in an important sense, the facts which could be photographed."

Riis's words were vivid; his photographs were even more vivid. They proved beyond doubt the truth of what he had been writing about slum conditions. "From them there was no appeal," he wrote. "I had at last an ally in the fight with the Bend."

6

Flowers
for
"The Poors"

> "The way to fight the slum in the
> children's lives is with sunlight and
> flowers and play."
> —*A Ten Years' War*

For nearly ten years Jacob Riis and his beloved Elisabeth
lived in South Brooklyn. Their home was small, and when
three children—Edward, Clara, and John—were added to
the family, it became altogether inadequate. Riis was a
home-loving man and he did not enjoy cramped quarters.
Neither did he like living in a thickly settled neighborhood that was constantly growing more crowded. The
small Danish town he had grown up in was surrounded
with fields and woods and water, and he loved the out of
doors. Every day his work took him to the worst and
most crowded part of New York City. "The deeper I
burrowed in the slum," he said, "the more my thoughts
turned, by a sort of defensive instinct, to the country."

Whenever possible, Riis took his family for walks in
the big park near their home and on outings into the
country. Sometimes he would strike out on a longer walk
by himself. One Sunday, on such a walk, he discovered

an open part of western Long Island that still had meadows and woods and streams. This community of Richmond Hill also had a railroad that connected with the New York City 34th Street ferry across the East River. What an ideal place to have a home!

With his usual impetuosity Jacob Riis picked out lots the very next week and, using determination and ingenuity in place of ready money, managed to buy them. It helped when, just then, he had a chance to earn two hundred dollars by assisting an insurance company to revise its Danish policies, and when a friend agreed to build the house, taking a mortgage for its cost. This mortgage did not worry Riis; his philosophy was that if he did the best he could about anything, it was bound to turn out right.

Within a few months the Richmond Hill house was ready. The family joyfully moved into what was to be their home for many years. "A blessed, good home," Jacob Riis called it, with "a wife who fills the house with song, and the laughter of happy children about me."

The Riis home stood on a ridge of wooded hills and had "a tangle of trees" around it. Robins and orioles nested in them; so did the starling with its "sweet, whistling notes"—a bird Riis had loved as a boy in Denmark. The lilac bushes were filled with honeybees and there was a place for a garden. Soon another daughter, Kate, was added to the household. There were also many pets, for all the family loved animals. At one time they had a horse, a pony, a dog (Bruno), several cats, rabbits, and pigeons.

In this "blessed, good home" Riis relaxed in the evening after the long day of strenuous work, which, he admitted, "takes all the spunk there is in me." Whenever he was

44

home at the time the children were being put to bed, he would sit beside them and tell them bedtime stories, usually about animals and often continued from session to session. Always they were absurd, imaginative, suspenseful, and full of delight for the children.

Many of the old Danish customs were followed in this Richmond Hill home, especially at Christmas, which to Riis was "ever the dearest [day] in the year." The traditional Danish dinner was served, with roast goose stuffed with apples and prunes, apple cake, and rice pudding with cinnamon and sugar and a single almond for luck. A tree, shining with candles and glowing with oranges, red apples, and colored-paper cornucopias, stood in the parlor. Joining hands, the family danced about it, singing the familiar Christmas carols. One Christmas Eve, Jacob hitched the horse to an old wagon and drove a load of happy children and grownups about the neighborhood, all singing carols at the top of their voices, although he claimed that he himself could not carry a tune.

At the far end of the backyard Riis built a little study in a cluster of trees. Here he wrote various articles, which he sold to several New York newspapers. They were intended both to stir the social conscience of New Yorkers and to help pay the mounting household bills. He told stories of pickpockets, tramps, and thieves; told them with compassion and often with humor. He related heroic deeds of firemen and police, and even of criminals. His rare ability to combine firsthand knowledge with a sensitiveness for human feelings made these anecdotes of actual happenings memorable reading. A writer, trying to describe Riis's "basic stylistic technique," called it "the short vignette," and said that his method was "to begin

45

with a quick, dramatic statement of a person's plight, then to reveal the tension between the relentless struggle for survival and the quick emotions of love, anger, greed, and friendship . . . closing with an appeal to the reader's sense of justice." If Riis was not the first, he was certainly one of the first to develop and popularize the "human-interest" newspaper story.

One sunny June morning the three elder Riis children were out in the fields early, picking daisies. They came in before their father left for the city and, thrusting great armfuls of the fresh field flowers into his hands, begged him to take them with him and give them to "the poors."

He did, and was overwhelmed by the sensation they caused. Before he had walked a half block from the ferry, he was surrounded by children who went wild over the common little field flowers. They implored him to give them some of the "posies," even if only just one blossom. When the flowers were gone, the children who failed to get any "sat in the gutter and wept with grief."

Their emotion over the flowers so touched Riis that, when he reached his office empty-handed, he sat down at his desk and wrote a letter to several newspapers. With something like a touch of genius he described his experience and suggested that some of the other thousands of commuters from the country to the city might like to share it. If they would bring an armful of flowers to town, "the pleasure of giving the flowers to the urchins who will dog their steps on the street, crying with hungry voices and hungry hearts for a 'posy,' will more than pay for the trouble." Those who could not bring in the flowers themselves might like to send them to his office at 303 Mulberry Street. Riis promised he would gladly distribute any that came in. The fifty doctors whom the Health Department assigned to the district for the summer months would help, he was sure. "Let us have the flowers!" Riis ended his letter.

To his astonishment the response was terrific. Flowers appeared in bunches, bags, baskets, buckets, boxes, and barrels. They came around the clock, brought by pedestrians, by bicycle, cart, wagon, and the railway express. "Express wagons carrying flowers jammed Mulberry Street, and the police came out to marvel at the row." Flowers arriving from near and far soon flooded not only Riis's office but the whole press building with their fragrance. Not only the Health Department doctors but rival reporters and the astonished policemen willingly took a hand in their distribution.

Everyone on Mulberry Street and the streets roundabout—the old as well as the young—seemed to want a flower. Children came "running breathless with desperate entreaty: 'Oh, mister! give *me* a flower.'" And everywhere the flowers went it was noticed that a new note of courage and of harmony appeared. "Fretful babies stopped crying and smiled. . . . Slovenly women courtesied and made way. . . . The worst street became suddenly good and neighborly." Riis said, "I have seen an armful of daisies keep the peace of a block better than a policeman and his club."

One of the most generous contributors of flowers was a religious women's organization called the King's Daughters. When the flowers continued to pour in until Riis could no longer cope with the situation, he appealed to this organization to take over. The King's Daughters responded by setting up a center in the basement of a tenement not far from Riis's office. As they distributed flowers, they also encouraged mothers and children to brighten dreary homes with a house plant or two or a window box. These devoted women became so conscious of the plight of the slum-dwellers that they hired a nurse to help them with their physical problems. Gradually the organization's activities expanded, and from the basement room it moved to 50 Henry Street and became King's Daughters' Settlement House.

Settlement houses were just then beginning to appear in New York, marking the beginning of a growing social-service movement. Congenial groups of men and women who wanted to help their fellowmen make better lives for themselves would rent a building in a poor section of the city and live there as friendly neighbors. Most of the volunteers were young men and women, many of them recently graduated from college. A large number of them had been inspired by the example of Toynbee Hall, the first social settlement, established in the poorest, most squalid section of London, England. Its aim was to help improve conditions by first becoming better acquainted with the neighborhood and gaining the confidence of its people, then seeking ways to relieve their misery and solve some of their problems.

Jacob Riis played a large part in the life of the early New York settlements. He believed they should first gain an understanding of their special neighborhood, then set to work to have an active impact on it. "Neighbor is the password," he declared. "Neighbor—that is all there is to it." He gladly gave advice, encouragement, and actual physical help as settlement leaders set up nurseries, opened kindergartens and playgrounds, equipped small

48

gymnasiums, and organized clubs and classes for young people and adults. They consulted him so often about their various projects that they laughingly called him their "volunteer auxiliary."

Riis told of a settlement Christmas party where he played Santa Claus and handed out two hundred dolls dressed by the settlement house volunteers and their friends for the little girls of the neighborhood. One of them tried to pawn her doll because her mother was sick and her father had run away. The pawnbroker, angry at being offered a mere doll, smashed it. When Riis heard of this he was furious. In telling the story he said vehemently, "I am no scrapper [though some might have thought otherwise] . . . but I own that the notion of having just one little round with that man, just one little one, has charms that I cannot get around."

The City of New York did not provide the recreational and educational opportunities needed by the people of the tenement-house district. Nor, as Riis was quick to point out, did the way most of these slum-dwellers were forced to live help them to become healthy, intelligent American citizens. Settlement houses tried to meet this need. Since immigrants naturally settled among their own kind, the Lower East Side was made up of clannish neighborhoods of Irish, Italians, and Jews, as well as of Negroes, Chinese, and other minority groups. The classes and clubs of the settlement houses were open to all, whatever their nationality, race, or religion. Settlement workers tried hard to remove the barriers that existed among the different groups and to create a community spirit. The Neighborhood Guild, one of the earliest settlements in New York, for example, formed a street-cleaning association whose members agreed to be responsible for keeping clean a single block—their own. The Guild provided containers for wastepaper, ashes, and garbage. This was only one of the ways in which settlements tried to encourage people to help themselves—a prize objective with all social workers. As Riis remarked, "When we fight no longer *for* the poor but *with* the poor, the slum is taken in the rear and beaten already."

But first, he realized, slum conditions must be improved to a point where the people had the physical stamina and moral will to fight for themselves. "One must begin with the conditions of life against which his [the slum-dweller's] very existence is a protest," he wrote.

Mortality statistics showed beyond doubt that filthy tenements were breeding places for disease—literally "dens of death." Lillian Wald, a courageous and humane professional nurse, was so moved by the sickness and misery in the homes of the very poor that she started a visiting-nurse service to relieve their suffering and to educate them in more sanitary and healthful ways. She and Riis knew each other well; she mentions him in her book, *House on Henry Street,* in which she describes her work.

Every effort to help the people of the tenements won Jacob Riis's hearty support. He did all he could to help others campaign against poverty. But he also fought his own particular war against the slums in his own particular way. "I was ever an irregular," he wrote, "given to sniping on my own hook." The special battle he was engaged in was his "death grapple with . . . the Bend," and this he vowed to fight through to victory.

7
"How the Other Half Lives"

"I like to set down what I see as
truly as I can."
—*Sunday School Times*,
July 5, 1902

The "Mulberry Bend crank" was having money troubles. His salary was not large and his home expenses were. He was "not good at figures; a child could do better," he said, but he did not need to be an accountant to see that his household bills were getting the best of him. Going without lunches did not make much difference. The brief articles he wrote for various newspapers—the *Journal*, the *World*, the *Mercury*—helped a little, but not enough. Somehow he must bring in more money. But how? Since magazines paid better rates than newspapers, Riis tried selling illustrated articles to them, but all he had for his efforts were a few nibbles for some of his photographs.

He thought of the stereopticon machine, the "magic lantern" that had come to his aid once years ago. Why not have slides made of some of his photographs and work up an illustrated lecture? The idea of such a lecture appealed to him. He could call it "How the Other Half

Lives." Church groups should be interested in such a presentation; it might arouse young people to do something for their city's desperately poor. And it should help the family exchequer.

No sooner thought of than acted upon. Riis went over his photographs with care and selected a large number of dramatic, storytelling pictures. He had slides made of them, then set to work to build a talk around them. In it he used both human-interest stories and significant facts about New York's poor. When all was ready, he approached various church organizations in Manhattan and Brooklyn. To his dismay, they were not in the least interested. After some of his photographs had appeared in the *New York Sun,* however, the City Mission did invite him to lecture at the Broadway Tabernacle. It was a moderate success and a few other churches opened their doors to him.

In one of the church audiences there happened to be an editor from *Scribner's Magazine.* He was so deeply impressed with Riis's slides and with his message that he went to the *Tribune* office on Mulberry Street to talk with him. Would he, the *Scribner* editor asked, be interested in using his material to write an article for *Scribner's?*

Would he! Riis was delighted. Not only would publication in a "quality" magazine like *Scribner's* pay more than the newspapers did; it would give him the chance to tell his story to a different and far broader audience. Much would depend on this first appearance in the magazine field. He must do a great job! He knew he was sometimes accused of exaggerating, but he would take care to keep this *Scribner* article low-keyed and entirely unsensational, and "not to overstate" his case. "I knew that it would be questioned, and was anxious that no flaws should be picked in it, for, if they were, harm might easily come of it instead of good."

It was February, 1889, when Riis started to write the article. All that spring and summer he worked on it whenever he could find the time. He hated to give up relaxing with his wife and children after a long, nerve-racking day's work in the city and instead to settle down to hours of writing. But he thought of the rewards and forced himself, evening after evening and weekend after weekend, to concentrate on the *Scribner* article.

For the most part he wrote in the little study in his backyard, but sometimes, late at night, with his family asleep upstairs, he would light the lamps in the downstairs rooms of the house and pace the floor, pipe in mouth, working out ideas and sentences. "I do most of my writing on my feet," he said later. Thoughts came to him, too, as on Saturday or Sunday he planted, transplanted, and hoed in his small garden—work he loved. His wife understood the importance of what he was doing and did not protest at his absorption in it, except when he seemed badly overtired.

Writing the magazine article was more difficult than working up lecture notes, even though the material was much the same. He wanted to describe dramatically yet realistically the "cheerless lives" of the poor living on New York's Lower East Side. He wanted to show how, unable to make a decent living, they were forced to exist in tenements where "dirt and desolation reign in the wide hallway and danger lurks on the rickety stairs." And he wanted to move his readers to action.

In the article Riis drew on his ten years of experience as a police reporter. He told story after story of cases he had seen personally. He described a garret room where a sick man and his wife slept on the floor, their older two children in boxes, and the baby in an old shawl hung from the rafters, while the winter winds howled through the roof. He mentioned a woman found dead on a bed of straw overrun with rats. He reported the suicide of a discouraged widow. Despair, he said, as well as disease, brought death in the slums, and "many forlorn lives ended in the river."

Riis touched, too, on the reasons for the high rate of crime in the slums. It was easy enough, he suggested, to slide into crime when rents were impossibly high, work hard to get, and then so underpaid that it sometimes took ten hours of steady labor to bring in twenty-five cents. Lack of honest, fairly paid jobs, he claimed, was sending thousands to asylums and workhouses where they became public charges.

He also had a word to say about the ever-present saloon. It was, he admitted, "too often the only cheerful, bright, and comfortable spot in the block," but it must share the blame, together with grasping landlords and employers, for many a poor man's downfall. Worst of all, he said, was the fate of the children who, with no room for them at home and no playgrounds anywhere about, were forced into the streets, where the police drove them off to gather in alleyways or on the waterfront and form into lawless gangs. It was the environment, Riis contended, that was mainly responsible for the difficulties of the poor, and it was society that was responsible for the environment.

54

"How the Other Half Lives: Studies among the Tenements" was the lead article in *Scribner's Magazine* for December, 1889. It spread over twenty pages and was illustrated with many drawings ("after the author's instantaneous photographs"). Among these were a typical rear tenement, Double Alley, the old-clothes section of an outdoor market, sleeping "street Arabs," and a five-cent lodging-room. The grim, dramatic pictures compelled attention, while the text, written in Riis's lively, informal style, and introducing many anecdotes that emphasized the plight of New York's poor, made irresistible reading.

The publication of this article was for Riis "the beginning of better days." Almost immediately invitations to lecture began to pour in from schools and social organizations—even from churches that had previously been uninterested. The most important result, however, was that the very week "How the Other Half Lives" appeared, Riis had a letter from an editor suggesting he expand the article into a book, which Scribner would be interested in publishing. This was almost more good fortune than the author was ready to cope with, but as usual he met the challenge.

Riis began work on the book on New Year's Day, 1890, and it was published in November of that year. With his full-time reporting job and frequent lecture engagements, he was free only on evenings and weekends to work on it. Over the years he had kept rather full notebooks, and most of the new material he needed he gathered from these and from scrapbooks of his newspaper stories. Statistics came from the New York Police and Health departments. Riis did not hold the handwritten pages until he completed the manuscript but sent each chapter to the publisher as soon as he had finished it.

That summer Riis left the *New York Tribune*, where he had been for twelve years, to work as an independent reporter, selling police news to all papers. Financially the move was a success, and he enjoyed the freedom of being his own man, but, what with writing the book and doing more lecturing, it was altogether too great a strain. Not surprisingly, working day and night and weekends, he became more and more overtired.

One evening he went to a Brooklyn church to give his lecture. Suddenly he realized he was sitting in the audience instead of being on the stage explaining the pictures being flashed on the screen. He quickly mounted the platform and began to speak. Luckily, in the darkened hall no one had seemed to notice the lapse.

Another time, having traveled to Boston to take part in an evening discussion on sweatshops, Riis went to call on a friend before the meeting. The friend was out, and Riis was asked to leave his name. His name? His mind suddenly went blank and he had to fumble in his pocket for his card. Being so dead tired he could not even remember his own name was not funny, he decided, and he had better do something about it. So he gave up the independent reporting and in November, on the very day his book came out, joined the staff of the *New York Evening Sun*.

A few weeks before this, Jacob Riis had appeared in his family living room waving a piece of paper—the last page of the last chapter of the book manuscript. He celebrated the end of his long, lonely task by turning a somersault. His wife beamed; Ed, John, and Clara clapped; and in her high chair little Kate crowed. Perhaps now the head of the house would pay a little more attention to his family; they had been neglected far too long!

The book, like the article that inspired it, was entitled *How the Other Half Lives* and carried the subtitle: *Studies among the Tenements of New York*. In the book Riis had room to expand many of the subjects and ideas he could only mention briefly in the magazine article. He wrote more about the racial strains that made up the Lower East Side, elaborating on the characteristic qualities of the Irish, Italian, Jewish, Bohemian, Negro, and Chinese peoples. Readers were amazed at the extent of his knowledge of them and of their adjustment to the new country and the progress they had made in it. He described the Jewish market, told of the Bohemian cigarmakers, and painted a vivid picture of the Italian sweatshop where a dozen men, women, and children worked in the same small room in which they cooked meals and washed and dried their clothes. He recounted the life of working girls whose wages were too low to live on, and drew unforgettable word pictures of the life of the street Arabs and other neglected children.

In the book, as in the magazine article, Riis blamed the saloons for much of the slum's vice and crime. The saloon, he said, "breeds poverty and corrupts politics, steals brains, ruins children." He explained how the slum-dweller, because he had so little cash, had to pay more for everything, buying his coal by the pail and his food in small quantities, and how, living from day to day and from hand to mouth, he had no incentive to look ahead. Yet most tenement tenants, Riis believed, had "instincts of cleanliness" and would respond favorably to better living conditions. Model tenements, he said, were urgently needed, along with more work and living wages.

How the Other Half Lives made a tremendous stir. People read it eagerly and recommended it to their friends. Social workers read and reread it and referred to it constantly. Clergymen quoted it in their pulpits. Overnight Jacob Riis became *the* authority on the New York slums.

In lengthy reviews the contents of the book were outlined and commented upon. The *Nation* thought that while Mr. Riis was "occasionally overcome by the appalling character of the sights that he has personally witnessed, his account of them is generally marked by sobriety and self-restraint." The review concluded: "In his view the tenement-house is the root of all evil, and the only hope of improving the characters of degraded human beings consists in improving their dwellings."

Reviewers frequently compared the book—sometimes favorably, sometimes unfavorably—to *In Darkest England,* a book about slum conditions in England, recently written by General William Booth, founder of the Salvation Army.

Later estimates of *How the Other Half Lives* recognized its importance even more than those written soon after its publication. Journalist Lincoln Steffens wrote in 1903 that "it awakened public conscience and was responsible for the appointment of investigating commissions and ten years of constructive fighting to improve the condition of the poor."

In his 1921 volume on Theodore Roosevelt in the Yale *Chronicles of America,* Harold Howland made the claim that *How the Other Half Lives* "did more to clean up the worst slums of the city than any other single thing."

In 1936, James Ford, in his authoritative *Slums and Housing,* called Jacob Riis "the first popular writer on the tenement-house problem to reach a national audience. . . . He, more than any other individual, succeeded in making apparent to the general public the needless horrors of slum life, and perhaps contributed more than any other to the public opinion which made possible the dramatic reforms at the beginning of the twentieth century."

In an introduction to Louise Ware's biography of Riis, published in 1938, the American historian, Allan Nevins, corroborates this, saying, "*How the Other Half Lives* let in a burst of light upon tenement conditions in New York, and did more than anything else to prepare the way for the housing investigations and new tenement-house codes of the next decade."

And the introduction to a 1970 edition of *How the Other Half Lives,* published by the Harvard University Press, states: "This is one of the great books of American journalism . . . for its impact on its generation and for the lasting ability to secure a reader's emotional assent to the vision of the author."

8

"Boss Reporter"
on
Mulberry Street

> "I did my work and tried to put
> into it what I thought citizenship
> ought to be."
>
> —*The Making of an American*

On the day Riis went over to the *Sun*—the day his book
How the Other Half Lives was published—the rival police
newspaper reporters finally acknowledged that "the
Dutchman" topped them all. After ten years of competi-
tive warfare, not all of it good-natured, he had won the
undisputed title of "boss reporter" on Mulberry Street.
It was, said Riis, "the only renown I have ever coveted or
cared to have."

In changing his paper, Riis had only to move upstairs
to the *Sun*'s office on the second floor of the police reporters' building. His policy of not belonging to any
combine of newsmen but playing it alone frequently gave
the *Sun* a lead on police news. So did his long working
hours. Early every morning as he approached the press
building he would call loudly for his helper, who was
now a young man named Max Fischel. Max would come
hurrying from Police Headquarters across the way,

where he had already noted the most important news items. Together they would climb the stairs, Riis would fling open his office window, and the two would sit down to study Max's notes. When they had decided which of them warranted investigation, the "leg work" would begin.

Much as he hated the slums where he worked, Jacob Riis thoroughly enjoyed his job. He liked people and was honestly interested in their problems. Writing was no great chore, for he found pleasure in working with words. And his ample sense of humor lightened the emotional strain of the frequently sordid, often tragic nature of his job. Try to cultivate your sense of humor, he once told some social workers; "it keeps the dream from spoiling." If there was anything funny in a situation, Riis was the man who could find it. He had a big rollicking laugh that could be heard—and often was—all over the building. But there was never anything mean or malicious in it.

Riis was one of those rare persons who can laugh at himself. He even relished relating some of the ridiculous mistakes he had made. Once, he said, he had described a river fire as if it had been on land, writing of "the mad gallop of horses, the crash and grinding of the heavy wheels that struck fire from the pavement" as the fire engines rushed to the scene. But he could laugh when it was pointed out to him that fireboats, not land equipment, were used to put out river fires. He admitted that in his eagerness to paint a vivid picture he had forgotten that fireboats as well as firehouses were listed in the city books as numbered companies.

He enjoyed telling about one hot summer day when he had tried to keep cool by spreading a cabbage leaf on his head under his hat before going out into the heat. His first call was on a bereaved household to get information on a tragic death in the family. To his shocked surprise the mourning ladies who greeted him at the door burst into hysterical laughter as he lifted his hat. He put his hand to his head, discovered the wilted cabbage leaf, and understood the laughter.

There were frequent breaks in the warfare among the reporters at 303 Mulberry Street. Some of these included laughing together at the antics of Trilby, a mongrel dog they had rescued from a gang that had tied a tin can to her tail and were chasing her. After her rescue, Trilby made the reporters' part of Mulberry Street her headquarters. She made herself at home in their offices, rode the elevator in the police building across the street, and paid regular calls on the police officers, even the chief. Sometimes on quiet days she would stand outside the reporters' building and sing—only one note, said Riis, "but it made up in volume what it lacked in range. Standing in the circle of her friends she would raise her head until her nose pointed straight toward the sky and pour forth her melody with a look of such unutterable woe on her face that peals of laughter always wound up her performance, whereupon Trilby would march off with an injured air and hide herself in one of the offices."

One of Riis's sleuthing successes that helped win for him the title of "boss reporter" involved solving the mystery of seventeen cases of poisoning. According to the Health Department report, all the victims had precisely the same symptoms, though the six different doctors who had been consulted had given different diagnoses. By calling at the victims' homes Riis discovered that all of them had attended the same party and eaten from the same batch of ham sandwiches. He then called on the six doctors and put them in touch with one another. His information and their conversations resulted in their changing the various diagnoses to a single one—trichinosis, a disease caused by eating undercooked pork. Riis reported the revised diagnosis in his newspaper story. The other reporters, who had given the doctors' earlier diagnoses, tried to break down Riis's story but could make no headway against the doctors' final statement and that of the Health Department. So Riis won another round in the police reporters' perpetual contest of wits.

Jacob Riis's biggest "beat" came in the summer of 1891, when he exposed pollution in New York City's water supply. It started when, in checking the Health Department's weekly analysis charts, he noticed a mention of "a trace of nitrates" in the city water. This sounded suspicious to him and, on inquiring, he learned that what it meant in plain words was sewage contamination. For months there had been fear of a cholera epidemic in New York; now this threat of pollution seemed to him to make matters more alarming. He decided it must be investigated.

Riis's first move was to use the *Sun* to warn New Yorkers to boil their drinking water. Then, taking notebook and camera equipment, he set out for the source of the city's water supply. While other papers were loudly ridiculing the *Sun*'s boil-your-water precaution, Riis was tramping about the Croton River watershed sixty miles north of the city. He spent a week there, following to its source every stream whose waters flowed into the Croton River. Whenever he found evidence of pollution, he took a picture; in all he took dozens. Back in New York he wrote—and the *Sun* printed, along with many pictures— a five-column article entitled: "Some Things We Drink."

The public was aroused. (So, needless to say, were the rival papers and their scoffing reporters.) The city's Board of Health quickly dispatched inspectors to the Croton area. When they returned, they stated that conditions were even worse than had been reported in the *Sun*. They had seen bathing, swimming, and dog-washing going on in the Croton watershed rivers, refuse piled along their banks, and, worst of all, town sewage dumped directly into the water destined to be drunk by New Yorkers.

The rival New York papers could not refute Riis's story, bolstered as it was by photographs and upheld by the Board of Health inspectors. But they still insisted there was no danger, since running water purified itself. Riis investigated this theory. He consulted scientists to find out how long bacilli could live in running water, and he consulted engineers to find out how long water took to reach New York from a point sixty miles upstream. Then, carefully and calmly, he reported his findings. Bacilli, he wrote, could live for seven days in running water; it took only four days for water to reach New York from a point sixty miles upstream.

The upshot of Riis's investigation and stories in the *Sun* was that New York City had to buy property along the Croton River and the streams emptying into it and not only clean them up but revise the city's whole water-supply system. It cost a staggering amount—millions of dollars—but all agreed this was cheap compared to a possible cholera epidemic. In the process of the large expenditures politicians in Albany, said Riis, "took a hand. What is there they do not exploit?" One of them asked Riis years later how much he got out of it all. "Nothing," Riis answered. The politician did not believe him, but it was true. Single-handed, with no profit to himself and no special thanks from the public, Jacob Riis had been responsible for bringing pure water to New York City.

Riis was never one to rest on his laurels. Author of a successful book, firmly established as "boss reporter" on Mulberry Street, a popular lecturer, and a prolific magazine writer, he took no time out for self-congratulation. His sense of "mission," this compulsion to awaken the public to its responsibility for the city's poor, was constantly pushing him. He was active in the social-reform movements of settlement houses and of civic leaders. Through his writing he was influencing many hundreds of New York citizens and, more than he knew, he was also making people all over the country feel a concern about the plight of the poor in their communities.

When Jacob Riis was asked when he first became interested in improving social conditions, he recalled that when he was a boy in the little town of Ribe, Denmark, there was in it a single tenement house—a two-story, very bedraggled-looking place known as Rag Hall. One Christmas the small Jacob gave his own gift of a small silver coin to one of the Rag Hall tenants to spend on his ragged children. "The meanness and squalor of his home had somehow offended my boyish soul," Riis wrote years later, "whereupon I took over the job of brightening their lives with the distinct proviso that before making Christmas happy for the children, he should clean up and set his house to rights. . . . It was social reform upon a minute scale."

Now, as an adult, Riis took Mulberry Bend as his particular area of activity. "I was bound to kill the Bend, because it was bad," he said. He finally prodded City Hall into condemning most of the worst buildings, then was distressed at the slowness of the Mulberry Bend demolition. It was, he said, "official indolence that delayed its demolition nearly a decade after it had been decreed." Indeed, a City Hall man told Riis that the reason for the delay was that "no one down there [at City Hall] had been taking any interest in the thing."

Jacob Riis had no desire to get involved in politics. But he firmly believed that getting Mulberry Bend torn down was the first step toward wiping out the city's worst den of vice and crime and providing better living conditions for the people of the slum. This action, he could see, was dependent on having an honest and concerned city government, and that was something New York did not have.

For years New York had been controlled by a group of politicians known as Tammany Hall. Much earlier its leader had been Boss Tweed, a state senator who had been notorious for buying votes right and left in order to keep in power, and for stealing hundreds of thousands of dollars from the New York City treasury. The present Tammany leaders were almost as bad. They tolerated and even encouraged all sorts of lawbreaking in return for votes and money. Posing as friends of the poor, they would sometimes free down-and-out men from legal entanglements, find them jobs, and even lend them money, counting on their support and votes as return payment. The Tammany government, Lincoln Steffens said, was "bad government; not inefficient, but dishonest." It was, he wrote, "corruption by consent."

"I did not like boss politics," Riis said. He abhorred dishonesty and he had no patience with slick, so-called diplomatic methods. Outspoken and frequently short on tact, he antagonized politicians by confronting them with their failure to keep promises; he angered officials by bringing to their attention cases of bribery and inefficiency; and he made outright enemies of greedy landlords and businessmen who profited by keeping things the way they were.

Upheld by his dream of a better Mulberry Bend, a better New York City, and a better country, Jacob Riis fought on—with others when he could, alone when he must. "I could not stand by and see the Republic built on a pigsty," he declared. He was certain he would win eventually. "When a thing is right, it is bound to come, if we make it come." His dream was a Mulberry Bend where poor people could live with pride, with a park in its center where the sun would shine down on happy children who at last would be given their right to play.

9
For the Children

"Real reform of poverty and
ignorance must begin with the
children."

—*The Children of the Poor*

From the day Jacob Riis went to Mulberry Street the
children of the tenements filled a very special place in his
heart. He saw them—dirty, ragged, sore-eyed but gay-
spirited—leapfrogging over the hydrants, dancing to the
music of the occasional hurdy-gurdy, picking fights with
outsiders and with one another. He also saw the sad-faced
boys and girls who leaned against old buildings or shrank
back in doorways, listless from lack of food, some of
them covered with bruises from beatings by drunken
parents.

The boys and girls who swarmed over the streets were
driven off by the police—for their own safety as well as
to permit the horse-and-wagon traffic. They would disappear, shouting names at the police, whom they regarded
as their natural enemy; then in a few moments many of
them would be back again. There was no place for them
in their miserable homes, no room or welcome in many
of the public schools, and no playground for miles
around. No wonder, Riis thought, they formed into
gangs and soon were in trouble with the law.

Jacob Riis was not on Mulberry Street long before he
began his "years of nagging at reluctant officials" to lay

68

out small parks in crowded tenement districts. Did they not realize that three hundred thousand people on the Lower East Side lived out of sight and out of reach of any "spot of green"? It was the city's responsibility, he told them at City Hall, to provide recreational facilities for its children. "The only way to fight the slum in the children's lives is with sunlight and flowers and play. . . . Boys have to yell to be healthy. Unless they have the chance, they are likely to turn out either wicked or dull." But the warnings fell on deaf ears and his nagging went on for years before anything happened in the way of parks.

Meanwhile, Riis reminded them, the city was paying heavily to maintain, though in a poor way, reform institutions filled with young minor criminals made by the street. "Idlers are in training for the penitentiary," he informed officials. And he insisted that it took very little to turn them into "toughs," and even less to turn the toughs into criminals.

"The tough," said Riis, "with all his desperation, is weak rather than vicious. . . . At first he rather enjoys the wild life of the streets; he soon gets caught up in a maze of minor lawbreaking. He learns how to rob tills, raid groceries, and eventually becomes a bold, clever thief, a fighter, and often a murderer." He went on to warn: "We have the choice of hailing him as man and brother, or of being slugged and robbed by him." And he said earnestly, "No investment gives a better return today on the capital put out than work among the children of the poor."

By working with settlements Riis tried to help provide for children and young people of the Lower East Side the recreational opportunities the city did not furnish. He found, as he told others, that it paid off well. Theodore Roosevelt agreed. He wrote: "When I was a police commissioner I found (and Jacob Riis will back me up in this) that the establishment of a boxing club in a tough neighborhood always tended to do away with knifing and gun-fighting among the young fellows who would otherwise have been in murderous gangs. Many of these young fellows were not naturally criminals at all, but they had to have some outlet for their activities."

The "murderous gangs" were as well known to the police reporters as to the police. Among them were the Pot Ashes, the Dutch Mob, the Stable Gang, and Mulberry Bend's own gang, the Whyos. When not occupied with their acts of violence against outsiders, these gangs were busy fighting one another. It was the street with its idleness, Riis insisted, that was largely responsible for making criminals of these boys.

The smaller Mulberry Bend children were quick to recognize Jacob Riis as their friend. In summer they would run to meet him as he walked to work from the East River ferry, his arms still often filled with flowers. He did not ask for particulars when a group of ragged children knocked on his office door and asked for some daisies "for a lady in the back." He learned later that they had wanted them to decorate the pine-board casket of a crippled old woman lying in a rear room waiting for the city hearse. It seemed she had always had a kind word for children.

Riis took a happy, simple pleasure in playing with children, both his own and the ragged urchins of Mulberry Bend. In winter, when the streets were slippery

70

with ice and snow, he confessed that he never could resist a slide down one of them, joining with an "unending
string of boys and girls going down it with mighty
whoops . . . at the risk of literally going down in a
heap with the lot."

It was not the flowers, the play, or the occasional
candy or penny from his pocket that endeared Jacob Riis
to the children of the tenements. They could see the
kindness in the plain face beneath the slouch hat and
knew instinctively that, as Lincoln Steffens said, "he
cared." They could bring him their troubles, certain of
his quick understanding and of his readiness to help.

It was impossible for Riis to turn his back on misery.
Whatever the difficulty, he would go out of his way to
try to correct it. Sometimes it was a family of helpless
children whose father had deserted them and whose
mother was dying of consumption. It could be a pair of
parents searching frantically for a lost child. Or it might
be a family with young children, evicted for lack of rent
money. Riis ran himself ragged for all of them. "He
fought for the weak," said Theodore Roosevelt, "he
fought against corruption in high places; but perhaps the
fight that was closest to his heart was the fight for
children."

Much manufacturing, especially the production and
finishing of clothing, was done in tenement homes. Here
children worked long hours in cramped, airless rooms
often at tasks beyond their strength. In these sweatshops
children were taught as soon as their little hands could
manage it to pull basting threads, turn hems, sort feathers,
cut out embroidery, make artificial flowers. Sometimes
they sat beside their mothers or older sisters, who were

bent over sewing machines or straining their eyes making buttonholes or finishing pants—at something like thirty cents a day. Many parents depended on their children's help to pay the rent; sometimes the children contributed as much to the family income as the adults.

All this troubled Riis deeply. It worried him, too, that in many sweatshop families parents evaded the law that forbade small children working. They not only did this themselves, but they trained their children to do the same, hiding when inspectors called or lying about their age. If a case of scarlet fever or some other contagious disease was reported and the health inspector ordered work stopped, the "sweaters" would put aside their work until he left, then begin again. The risk of spreading disease meant little to them; the necessity to go on with their task, everything. If they did not work, they were afraid there would be no food in their mouths and no roof over their heads.

Conditions in the factories were no better. A law had been passed prohibiting the employment of anyone under fourteen; certificates were required of minors, giving dates and places of birth. But false certificates were easy to get. Unscrupulous notaries made them out for a quarter each, or sometimes for nothing, for some political reason. Overseers in factories whisked the underage children out of sight whenever an inspector arrived. All this deceit, Riis pointed out, was training young people to lie and to have no respect for law.

Riis, investigating on his own, found that many of the children working in factories could not speak English and had never been to school. Some attended night school, where they gave their true ages, which were under fourteen. Besides getting little or no schooling, the children's health was being undermined by their confining work. Inspections, Riis felt, should be more rigorous, and instead of requiring work certificates, which could so easily be faked, birth certificates should be required, or parents' passports, which gave the children's birth dates.

Riis was concerned, too, about young women who worked in stores and factories. Their wages were pitiably low and their working hours painfully long. When a bill was pending in the state legislature to shorten the hours of working girls, Riis spoke at a meeting at the Cooper Union, making a forceful speech to urge its passage.

Two years after the success of *How the Other Half Lives,* Riis's second book, *Children of the Poor,* was published. In it he stated his belief that it was the duty of the state to provide a healthy environment for boys and girls to grow up in. He argued that this would work to the advantage of the state as well as the children, since the environment in which the young lived determined the kind of men and women they would become and so the kind of government the state would have when, as adults, they took over its control. How could children be expected to learn "American ways and the self-respect of future citizens and voters," he asked, if they lived in dark, disease-ridden tenements, had no place to play, and instead of going to school were forced into the street or put to work in a factory or sweatshop? And again he pointed out there was not a single park below 14th Street, where at least fifty were needed.

In *Children of the Poor,* Riis put over his points by

73

telling story after story of children he had known. He told of the nine-year-old girl who worked from seven in the morning until eight at night to add a dollar a week to the family funds. . . . Of boys who picked over cinders and sorted out rags at the river dump where carts unloaded their refuse. . . . Of Giuseppe, a ragged newsboy who crawled into a basement ventilator chute to keep warm and was burned to death when a fire broke out. . . . Of solemn, crippled Pietro who, when asked if he never laughed, thought it over and replied soberly, "I did wonst."

Again Riis emphasized his faith in facts. It was facts, not theories, he wrote, that were needed to right the wrongs in the slums. For years he had been gathering these facts and now he was setting them down in *Children of the Poor* in the hope that others would take them and build upon them. Riis's dedication read: "To my children who come rushing in from the autumn fields, their hands filled with flowers 'for the poor children' I inscribe this book. May the love that shines in their eager eyes never grow cold within them; then they shall yet grow up to give a helping hand in working out this problem which so plagues the world today."

Richard Gilder, editor of the *Century Magazine*, had become one of Riis's close friends. He was active in social-reform movements and was chairman of the commission appointed by the state legislature in 1894 to investigate and set up standards for New York City tenement houses. Riis wrote him a letter full of practical suggestions, such as making a colored map of nationalities living in the tenement-house area and choosing a representative from each to inquire into needed changes; he also recommended consulting Samuel Gompers, head of the American Federation of Labor. Mr. Gilder appreciated Riis's suggestions and encouraged him to write for the *Century*. In the fall of 1894, a startling article by Riis, entitled "The Making of Thieves in New York," appeared in it.

In this article Riis stated the need for more and better schools in the city. He said he had changed his mind about the tenements being entirely to blame for child criminals. Schools, he now saw, were equally at fault. The lack of room in the New York schools, which drove boys and girls into the streets, must take the responsibility for their turning up in police courts "younger and tougher." Officially called truants, these young people were often jailed for minor offenses along with the scum of city life—vagrants and beggars, burglars and pickpockets. These young "criminals," said Riis, were "the victim of evil associations, of corrupt environment. They were not thieves by heredity; they were made. And the manufacture goes on every day. The street and the jail are the factories."

Statistics showed, said Riis, that eight times as many criminals came from among those who could not read or write as from among those who could. This being the case, would the city not find it both cheaper and better to build schools than jails? Public schools should be "the real cornerstone of our liberties" and provide children with at least enough education so they would grow "to the stature of responsible citizenship" and have the ability to vote intelligently. Good citizenship was of tremendous importance to this non-native-born American!

In this *Century* article Riis cited statistics to show that New York had not nearly enough schools for all its children. It was, in fact, reaching hardly more than a third of them. In addition to using others' figures, Riis did considerable investigation himself, visiting school after school. One classroom was so crowded that the two pupils nearest the door had to get up to let him in. Practically all the schoolrooms he visited were dark, the air was "foul and unhealthy," and the children, he wrote, were growing up crooked for want of proper desks.

One teacher admitted to Riis that she had a waiting list of two hundred. "Where are they now?" Riis asked, and answered his own question: "In the street, learning to become thieves." Teachers, he claimed, discouraged the dirty, shoeless children from coming to school, and the twelve truant officers employed by the city did only a halfhearted job of trying to enforce the unenforceable compulsory attendance laws.

That same fall of 1894, *Century* published another devastating Riis article called "Playgrounds for the Schools." In it he exposed the lack of adequate play areas in and around New York schools. Dark basements with "countless iron posts and pillars" were used as playrooms in some schoolhouses. One used a "gloomy little well between the school and a big factory building." Riis advocated putting a play area around every public school. He visualized this as a sort of combination playground and small park—"a playground for the children and a breathing spot for the overworked mothers with their babies, as well as a place where the fathers may smoke their evening pipes."

He declared: "When there is room for every boy on the school bench, and room to toss a ball when he is off it, there will not be much left of that problem [child crimes] to wrestle with." And he urged: "Build schools, give them playgrounds, decent houses—in short, give the children a chance."

10

Teddy and Jake— "Brothers in Mulberry Street"

> "I loved him from the day I first saw him."
>
> —*The Making of an American*

Citizens of New York, many of them aroused by Riis's *How the Other Half Lives*, were beginning to realize that their city government was impossibly corrupt and must be changed. They were startled when, in February, 1892, Dr. Charles Parkhurst, a prominent New York clergyman, courageously denounced from the pulpit the crime that flourished in the city "with the connivance of the public authorities." Challenged by politicians and others to prove his accusations, Dr. Parkhurst produced a flood of evidence. New Yorkers were aghast. They could no longer turn their backs on the corrupt practices they now knew beyond doubt were going on in city departments. Led by Dr. Parkhurst, they formed various reform organizations and began a crusade for clean city government. The state legislature cooperated by appointing a commission—the Lexow Commission—to investigate New York City's Police Department.

Jacob Riis was in the thick of everything. He reported

meetings of the reform organizations at length and wrote scathing stories for the *Sun* and other papers about blackmail, graft, fraudulent ballots in city elections, inefficiency and corruption in city government, and police protection of gambling places, saloons, and houses of prostitution. Always he had at hand the facts to support his charges.

Many friendships grew out of Riis's association with civic leaders during this period. Some who had been mere acquaintances became close friends, among them Dr. Felix Adler, Bishop Henry Potter, Dr. Jane E. Robbins, Josephine Shaw Lowell, and Richard Gilder. Dr. Adler had headed the 1884 tenement-house commission whose meetings Riis had reported. His slogan, "Deed, not creed," was also Riis's philosophy. Mrs. Lowell had founded the Charity Organization Society to prevent the overlapping of relief agencies and was its head. She and Riis were appointed to the Committee on Vagrancy, a subcommittee of the Lexow Commission. Dr. Robbins was connected with the College Settlement. There were others—so many that Riis once gratefully remarked that his life was "full of friendships that make it worthwhile."

With so many important, intelligent citizens actively battling for municipal reform, the movement could hardly fail. At a mass meeting in Madison Square Garden the findings of the Lexow Commission were made public. These confirmed the graft and dishonesty in the Police Department. A "Committee of Seventy" was elected to lead in the reform, and William Strong was endorsed for mayor of New York. In the 1894 fall election the reform forces won and William Strong was elected reform mayor of the city.

Mayor Strong made many changes, but the one that pleased Jacob Riis most was his appointment of Theodore Roosevelt as President of the New York Board of Police Commissioners. Riis had followed Roosevelt's career in the New York State Legislature and had admired the young man's exposure of bribery and his stand against boss rule. He had been enormously pleased when, not long after *How the Other Half Lives* was published, he had returned to his office one day and found Theodore Roosevelt's card with the words: "I have read your book and I have come to help." Soon the two men were fast friends.

Roosevelt said later that *How the Other Half Lives* had been to him "both an enlightenment and an inspiration for which I felt I could never be too grateful." He said that in it Riis had "drawn an indictment of the things that were wrong, pitifully and dreadfully wrong, with the tenement homes and the tenement lives of our wage-earners. In his book he had pointed out how the city government, and especially those connected with the departments of police and health, could aid in remedying some of the wrongs."

Despite their completely different backgrounds, Roosevelt and Riis were really much alike. Both were full of energy, though Riis was ten years older than Roosevelt, and both were highly unpredictable. They had the same great joy in life, the same keen sense of duty, the same sympathy for the underdog, the same driving determination to work for justice and humanity. Roosevelt said that he and Riis "looked at life and its problems from substantially the same standpoint. Our ideals and principles and purposes, and our beliefs as to the methods necessary to realize them were alike."

So when Roosevelt, the new head of police commissioners, appeared on Mulberry Street shouting "Hello Jake!" and asking "What do we do first?", it was no wonder that "Jake" felt a new day had dawned. Joyfully he escorted Roosevelt around the district, introducing him to officials, politicians, policemen, even rival reporters. He took him to meet Lillian Wald and other settlement-house leaders. He also introduced him to the world of the tenement slum.

Theodore Roosevelt did not flinch as they entered filthy halls, climbed flimsy stairways, and breathed the fetid air in rooms where whole families of "sweaters," lived and worked at finishing garments, making artificial flowers, or rolling cigars. He endured the stench of the loathsome courtyards with their unattached sewage pipes, their heaps of ragpickers' refuse and rotting garbage. He stepped over drunken tramps crouched in alleys and spoke to dirty children huddled in doorways.

Roosevelt and Riis made their inspection tours not only in the daytime but also in the middle of the night. In their after-midnight prowling about the streets they saw the worst side of tenement life and caught policemen off guard. Sometimes their encounters were funny, so funny that Riis could not resist sharing them with other reporters, who delightedly wrote them up in their newspaper columns. But the tours were important in showing what needed to be changed. The Lexow Commission had unearthed all kinds of irregularities and unlawful police practices; now Roosevelt saw these things for himself.

"The midnight trips that Riis and I took," said Roosevelt, "enabled me to see what the Police Department was doing, and also gave me personal insight into some of the problems of city life. It is one thing to listen in perfunctory fashion to tales of overcrowded tenements, and it is quite another actually to see what that overcrowding means, some hot summer night. . . . Much of it was heartbreaking, especially the gasping misery of the little children and of the worn-out mothers."

One of the first moves of the new President of the Board of Police Commissioners was to enforce the law requiring Sunday closing of saloons, "the chief source of mischief" in the slum. "Jake Riis and I spent one Sunday from morning till night in the tenement district, seeing for ourselves what had happened," Roosevelt said, and he wrote of the benefits of the Sunday saloon closing: "Savings banks recorded increased deposits and pawnshops had losses. . . . Husbands were now willing to take their families for an outing on Sunday."

Riis had a good deal to say about the "mischief" the saloon caused in the slum. Admitting that it was "bright and cheery and never far away," he argued that if tenement homes were pleasanter, the saloon would not be so popular. He liked to quote a legislative report: "To prevent drunkenness, give to every man a clean and comfortable home." It concerned him to see children exposed so constantly to the saloon. Even the smallest of them were sent to bring "growlers"—pitchers of beer—from the corner saloon. Too often Riis's plans for helping a man—and sometimes a woman—get a better job or a better place to live were undone by drunkenness.

Riis was all for helping the man who was down, but he

wrote: "It was and is an essential thing in a country like ours, not to prop him up forever, not to carry him, but to help him to his feet so he can go himself."

The Roosevelt-Riis friendship flourished. Lincoln Steffens reported in his *Autobiography* that everything in Riis's office was pushed aside when "Teddy" opened his second-story window at Police Headquarters and gave his famous *Hi yi yi!* cowboy yell to summon "Jake" from across the street. Riis's tremendous faith in Roosevelt grew, and so did the delight both men took in each other's companionship.

Although lamenting the slowness of the operation, Riis watched with satisfaction as one by one the ramshackle rear buildings of the Mulberry Bend slum were condemned and came tumbling down. The tramps had to find refuge elsewhere. No longer could hordes of them huddle in hallways and on stairways "in a shuddering double file that reached clear to the roof on rainy nights."

The tenants moved, too, many of them to four- and five-story buildings put up by private concerns and by public subscription. Most of these walk-ups had only four families to a floor, acceptable sanitary arrangements, a water supply on every floor, light and ventilation in inner rooms and halls, and watertight cellars.

With the move into more decent buildings the occupants began to take more interest in both their homes and their environment. A tenant, said Riis, is like a chameleon; he "takes on the color of his surroundings." Tenants became more aware of wrongs they had previously taken for granted and, encouraged by settlement-house workers, they would even protest such things as unclean streets, fire hazards, housing and factory violations, and child labor. Always Jacob Riis stood ready to expose injustices and to support all efforts to change things for the better.

While waiting impatiently for City Hall to complete tearing down the Mulberry Bend slum and construct in its place the promised Mulberry Bend Park, Riis concerned himself with the second "must" on his social-reform program. He had never forgotten the night he had spent as a penniless immigrant in a police lodging-room. He still shuddered as he recalled the policeman's clubbing to death the little dog that had waited for him all night on the police-station steps. For years he had nursed the idea of avenging the cruel deed. His hatred, however, had gradually shifted from the individual policeman who had done the deed to the whole police lodging-room system. Certain that it was wrong and that it encouraged vice and vagrancy, he battled against it, both alone and as a member of the Lexow Commission vagrancy committee. But he got nowhere.

Then, as he put it, "Theodore Roosevelt came, and destroyed the nuisance in a night." After inspecting several police lodging-rooms with "Jake" and hearing the story of his experience, Roosevelt was thoroughly aroused. He announced that the police lodging-rooms were a disgrace to the city and ordered them done away with. The "yellow" (sensational) newspapers accused Roosevelt of hardheartedness in condemning poor men to suffer on cold nights. They overlooked the fact that shelter for the needy was provided on an East River barge while a better system was being worked out. Roosevelt, as usual when he felt he was doing the right thing, paid no attention to his critics. Within a week of his order the police lodging-rooms were no more. Before long a decent municipal lodging shelter was set up "where a homeless man is treated like a human being" and where "intelligent inquiry" separated the needy from the imposters.

In the spring of 1896, Riis took on another responsibility. He became the executive officer, at a small salary, of the Good Government Clubs, a nonpartisan organization made up of sixteen individual clubs located in different parts of the city. This confederation represented five thousand New York voters pledged to work for municipal reform. Among its goals were "the elimination of bad housing, construction of small parks, amelioration of sweatshop and other bad labor conditions, improvement of the educational system, the erection of a truant school."

The aims were Riis's own, and for a year he devoted every moment he could spare to achieving them through the Good Government Clubs. He attended meetings, planned petitions, wrote lengthy letters, talked to state legislators and city officials. All this, added to everything else he was doing, proved to be an impossible program, and at the end of a year he was sensible enough to give it up. But in that one year under his leadership the Good Government Clubs could boast amazing accomplishments. "They made war," Riis reported, "upon the dark hall in the double-decker [a dark, airless type of tenement house] and upon the cruller bakery [the cause of many tenement fires]. They compelled the opening of small parks or the condemnation of sites for them anyway, exposed the abuses of the civil courts, the 'poor man's courts,' urged on the building of new schools, compelled the cleaning of the Tombs prison . . . took a hand in evolving a sensible and humane system of dealing with young vagrants . . . and compelled the enforcement of the existing tenement-house laws." They also obtained permission from the Board of Education to open up school buildings at night so that classrooms could be used for boys' clubs.

In many of these reforms Riis had the active assistance of his friend, Roosevelt. "No one ever helped as he did," said Riis. The two years, from 1895 to 1897, that Roosevelt was New York's President of the Board of Police Commissioners were perhaps the brightest in Jacob Riis's whole life. Then life was "really worth living, and I have a pretty robust enjoyment of it at all times," Riis said. It had been for him "the golden age," and at the time of Roosevelt's leaving he could foresee the return of Tammany Hall and City Hall corruption. "I knew too well the evil day that was coming back to have any heart in it [the slum reform]." Yet, though he had temporarily lost heart, he went valiantly on with his fight against the wrongs he saw around him.

The rubbish from the demolition of the Mulberry Bend buildings was left standing month after month. At last Riis could endure it no longer. To bring about action he drew up a formal complaint against the city (which now owned the property), for maintaining a nuisance that was "detrimental to health and dangerous to life . . . a mass of wreck, a dumping-ground for all manner of filth from the surrounding tenements. . . . The numerous old cellars are a source of danger to the children that swarm over the block. Water stagnating in the holes will shortly add the peril of epidemic disease."

Years before, when the Small Parks Act had been

passed, thanks to Riis's persistence, funds had been appropriated for a park on this site. City Hall had never been especially interested in the Mulberry Bend Park—it was Jacob Riis's private dream. But when some boys were accidentally killed while playing in a Mulberry Bend cellar hole, not long after Riis's arraignment, officials were roused to action.

By 1897, Mulberry Bend Park became a reality, and in June of the next year it was formally dedicated. A band played and speeches were made by political bigwigs. No one had thought to invite Jacob Riis to the platform. He stood modestly on the sidelines until one of his friends, catching sight of him, stepped forward and led the crowd in three rousing cheers for Jacob Riis, the man responsible for the whole thing.

The construction of this pleasant "spot of green," taking the place of the worst part of the Mulberry Bend slum, was to Riis probably the most satisfying accomplishment of his whole career. The Bend, he wrote happily, became "decent and orderly because the sunlight was let in, and shone upon children who had at last the right to play."

II

Reporting, Writing, and Roosevelt

> "Men, not money, make a country great."
>
> —*The Making of an American*

In the spring of 1897 Theodore Roosevelt went to Washington to become Assistant Secretary of the Navy. That fall, as Riis had feared, Tammany made a comeback, defeating Mayor Strong. "We were beaten," Riis said sadly. "Reform was dead and decency with it." Yet some of the gains made under Mayor Strong and his top police commissioner remained.

The friendship between Jacob Riis and the former President of the Board of Police Commissioners did not end with Roosevelt's departure from New York. In Washington, as rumors of Spanish outrages in Cuba were reported, "Teddy" rushed the United States Navy into readiness for war. Riis, swept up in the surge of humanitarian feeling, was "a hearty believer from the first" in the Spanish-American War. He spent several months in Washington working as a correspondent for his paper and, on the side, helping his friend Roosevelt speed up preparations for the conflict they both felt sure would come.

With the declaration of war, Roosevelt resigned his Navy post to organize a volunteer troop. Known as the Rough Riders, it was made up of Western cowboys, ranchers, and hunters, of Eastern college boys and New York policemen. When Roosevelt took them to Cuba to fight, Riis longed to follow. He could have gone as war correspondent for the *Outlook*, a magazine for which he had written articles, but he decided that his place was at home. He had lecture commitments, two of his children had scarlet fever, and his wife was frail. Both parents were upset because Ed, their oldest son, now a young man of twenty-one, had tried to enlist with the Rough Riders and John, at sixteen, had run away to join the Navy. Neither succeeded in his wartime ambition. For a time Jacob Riis sent dispatches about the Spanish-American War to a Copenhagen paper, but this arrangement did not last long. His reports, the Danish editor said, were too "ultrapatriotic" and too "youthful in their enthusiasm" for Denmark's neutral position.

Riis and his wife, who shared his admiration for Roosevelt, followed with intense interest the dispatches telling of the daring exploits of their Rough Rider hero. When they read of his valiant charge up San Juan Hill, the Riises gave two rousing cheers—"one for the flag and one for T. R." And when "Teddy" made his triumphal return to Washington, Jacob Riis was there to greet him.

Riis was writing and publishing more and more magazine articles. He and Richard Gilder, editor of the *Century Magazine,* had a close and happy association both personally and professionally. Altogether Riis wrote almost thirty articles for the *Century*. Most of them were concerned with the New York slums and slum-dwellers and many were quite lengthy.

Riis wrote many articles for the *Outlook* too; these were usually shorter than the *Century* ones. He also wrote for the *Forum*, the *Review of Reviews*, the *Survey*, the *World's Work*, and several other magazines. He even ventured into the juvenile field, doing "The Story of a New York Newsboy" for the *Youths' Companion* and "Slippers, the White House Cat," for *St. Nicholas*. Although the New York tenement-house district furnished the background for most of his articles, Riis also wrote about the New York firemen and police, a few semi-humorous stories of personal experiences, and numerous pieces on his friend Roosevelt.

It was perhaps surprising that Riis, who saw so much of the seamy side of life, still had a keen eye for beauty and could find it even in the midst of misery. He delighted in life's happy moments and enjoyed sharing those he encountered in the heart of the slum. In a *Century* article, "Feast Days in Little Italy," he described the picturesque celebration of saints' days in Mulberry Bend. He told of taking Roosevelt to a slum court where the people from a southern Italian village paid tribute to their patron saint. Sheets stretched over "outhouses and sheds" had converted the small court into a sort of temple and the tenement fire escapes along the alleys leading from Mulberry Street to it were so gaily decorated that they looked like festive balconies. Set against a rear tenement was a scarlet-and-gold shrine, festooned with ribbons and lit with candles; it held the life-size image of the saint, brought out from the saloon loft where, for a fee, it was stored from year to year. Italians of all ages—men, women, and children dressed in their holiday best—came to kneel before the shrine. Musicians, emerging from nearby saloons, "blew" Italian songs, including "Santa Lucia." A plate was passed around to collect the money needed to cover expenses, and in one corner a sheep, waiting to be raffled off, was surrounded by children pulling at its wool. Roosevelt took five shares, but lost; the sheep was won by a widow who, delighted by her unexpected good luck, hugged and kissed the animal before she led it away.

With his great love of Christmas, it was no wonder Riis delighted in writing about it. The celebration in the slums seemed to him especially touching. "Into the ugliest tenement street Christmas brings something of picturesqueness and cheer," he wrote. "Poor indeed is the home that has not its sign of peace over the hearth, be it but a single sprig of green." He tells of holly suspended from the lamp in a tenement hall that had been walled in to make room for a cobbler's bench and bed . . . of garlands of juniper, tamarack, or fir hung on mission- and settlement-house doors . . . of stray branches of hemlock, picked up at the grocer's, trimmed with a dime's worth of candy and tinsel and set in a pail for the children to dance about.

A tree he had helped to put up in a poverty-stricken room was still standing three weeks after Christmas because, the mother explained, "It looked so kind o' cheery-like there in the corner." . . . In one four-room attic occupied by three families and where each father's share of the rent was half his month's pay, a crib was fitted up

for the Nativity, with a doll for The Child. . . . Behind
the dirty window of a rear tenement a tiny tree, lighted
by three small candles, stood in a room black with dirt
and smoke; the oil stove, used for both heating and cooking, filled the middle of the room; the family wash,
"clammy and gray," hung on a line stretching across it.
Two children clapped their hands and wheeled the baby
in its old baby carriage closer to the little tree, while at a
table set with cracked dishes their discouraged mother
sat weeping. . . . In the pocket of a man picked up on
Christmas Eve for theft, the police found a child's scrib-
bled letter to Santa Claus. Touched by this evidence of
the man's reason for stealing, the police captain managed
his release and, with a few policemen helping, "made"
Christmas for the family. Then, best of all, he found a
job for the father. . . . Willie, a small newcomer to a
boys' lodging home, hung up an old stocking on the edge
of his bunk bed on Christmas Eve. The older boys, instead of laughing at him, took their hard-earned pennies
and while Willie slept went on a shopping spree to fill his
stocking.

At Mr. Gilder's suggestion, Riis collected some of the
Christmas and other human-interest stories of the slum
that he had written for newspapers and magazines and
made them into a little book. Called *Out of Mulberry
Street*, it was published in 1898. In the midst of preparing
it, Riis became "stalled" and had to rest a while before
going on. Doing so much writing, in addition to his newspaper reporting and all the social-reform work he was
constantly engaged in, plus giving frequent lectures, was
really getting to be too much! He was tempted to give
up the *Sun* job, but the regular salary was too important.

"The newspaper writing is my bread and butter," he wrote his foster sister Emma in Denmark.

When Roosevelt, back from Cuba, ran for the governorship of New York State in 1898, Riis helped him campaign. He admitted he was not very good at it, but he wanted to do what he could because he was so completely in sympathy with Roosevelt's campaign pledges. Some of these were to work for progress and social reform, to relieve tenement-house conditions, regulate sweatshop labor, and secure an eight-hour day for the workingman.

When Roosevelt won the office and moved to Albany, the overworked Riis began to take the train up the river to the state capital after office hours every few days. Riis simply disregarded fatigue if he felt he was accomplishing something worthwhile. Together the two men planned much of the legislation that was later passed to help improve the lives of the working men and women of the state. "Few were nearer to him [Roosevelt], I fancy, than I, even in Albany," he wrote.

Governor Roosevelt asked Riis to gather the facts about the sweatshops on New York's Lower East Side. Taking with him a union representative and three factory inspectors, he visited a large number of sweatshops, then made his recommendations. Among them were increasing the number of state inspectors and making night inspections.

"Once or twice," Theodore Roosevelt wrote in his *Autobiography*, "I went suddenly down to New York City without warning anyone and traversed the tenement-house quarters, visiting various sweatshops picked at random. Jake Riis accompanied me; and as a result of

93

our inspection we got not only an improvement in the law but a still more marked improvement in its administration."

One steaming hot day, Riis remembered, they visited twenty five-story tenements where "sweating" went on. They discovered many violations of the state law, which required that every room where there was any sort of manufacturing be licensed, and that it have "absolute cleanliness, no bed in the room where work was done, no outsider employed, no contagious disease, and only one family living in the room." Among other violations the Governor and Riis found that one tenement house, designed for seventeen families, was occupied by forty-three, with three families in every three-room flat, all cooking on the same stove. In one Italian home they stumbled upon a touching scene. The little daughter, dressed in white, with flowers and veil, was ready for her confirmation. They arrived as she bowed her head before her old grandmother to receive her benediction. Roosevelt spoke some kind words to them, then left. Riis followed him but could not resist turning back to whisper to the family the name of their distinguished visitor.

The *New York Times* reported the tenement-house inspection visit, commenting that this was the first time a governor of the state had ever made such a tour. Among its important results were the appointment by Roosevelt of more inspectors and the creation of a new tenement-house commission. Other social-reform legislation promoted by Roosevelt brought the installation of much-needed safety devices in factories, better regulation of sweatshop labor, reduced working hours for women and children, and laws to improve tenement-house conditions.

Riis was very sympathetic toward the efforts of the labor leaders to secure better pay and better working conditions for the laboring man. Although he encouraged the growth of the labor movement, he continually emphasized the importance of avoiding violence and of working within the law. After a strike during which violence had occurred, he wrote to his friend Dr. Jane Robbins of the College Settlement, "We can and will right our wrongs in an orderly way or the republic is a mockery."

12

Into the Twentieth Century

> "The walls . . . came down, as the
> walls of ignorance and indifference
> must every time, if you blow hard
> enough and long enough, with
> faith in your cause and in your
> fellowman."
>
> —*The Making of an American*

As the nineteenth century went out and the twentieth came in, Jacob Riis had reason to feel encouraged about many things. Working conditions were improving as trade unions grew stronger, child labor was beginning to disappear, factory and sweatshop controls were operating better. Best of all, the general public was now aware of the plight of the poor. Perhaps, New Yorkers began to say, the slum-dwellers—those practically unknown people in an almost unknown part of their own city—did not live the way they did from choice. Perhaps, as Jacob Riis and other pioneer social reformers kept pointing out, there really was a connection between bad living conditions and bad habits, health, morals, and crime. If that were so, then society certainly should try to improve those living conditions. And they, as members of society, ought to take a hand in the matter.

"Social science" was becoming a familiar term to most

Americans, and social work and social workers an every-day reality. Newspapers and magazines were calling attention to the need for improvement in the housing and working conditions of the nation's laborers. The United States Commissioner of Labor was putting out lengthy reports concerning the social problems of America's great cities.

In Boston a good start had been made providing parks in congested areas. But New York was, according to James Ford in his *Slums and Housing*, "the first American city to be aware of its housing problem." He credited this chiefly to the efforts of one man—Jacob Riis. By the early nineteen hundreds, private companies and social-minded organizations as well as the city of New York were building low-rent tenements. In the New York State Legislature a new and stronger law was being worked out to improve tenement housing. Everywhere agencies and organizations were being formed to study and work on the problems with which Jacob Riis had struggled almost singlehandedly for so many years.

The methods and procedures of the new "social action" workers naturally differed from the more personal ones Riis had used. The new patterns were more intricate and the coordination between organizations more complex. This did not bother Riis. Changing times, he agreed, called for changing remedies. "What are we," he said, "that we should think ourselves always right? . . . Let us go ahead and make our mistakes—as few as we can, as many as we must; only let us go ahead." So long, he might have added, as we move in the right direction.

He watched the people of the tenements becoming better and better able to help themselves. No longer were most of them fresh from Europe, ignorant of the language, the law, and the customs of the new country. The desperately poor whom he had known were turning into "lower-middle-class" citizens. Most of them were living in fairly decent homes; they had small parks to enjoy; and their children had new schools to attend. Their health was better, fewer babies were dying; the children had cleaner and sturdier bodies and happier faces. Riis also noted with satisfaction that their clothing was less ragged. The efforts of the pioneer social workers were paying off! With more understanding of American ways, the more ambitious immigrants were climbing up on the industrial ladder. "The immigrant boy easily outstrips in interest for his adopted home the native," Riis observed, and he noticed that the more thoughtful among the foreign-born were taking advantage of the books, newspapers, magazines, theaters, and musical opportunities increasingly made available to them.

But Jacob Riis still saw plenty to do. Too many of the tenements—and more than half of New York's population lived in tenements—were old and unacceptable by even minimum sanitary standards. Some buildings were so flimsy they had to lean on each other for support. Although most of the dark, airless, firetrap "double-decker" tenements were gone, the "dumbbell" type that had replaced many of them had grave faults. The air shaft, designed to carry up air, also carried up odors. Worse, in case of fire, it let flames rush upward. Progressive architects were experimenting with better designs, and progressive builders were putting up improved tenements that could be rented at a low figure and yet give the investor a reasonable profit. Some of the new buildings, instead of being built on narrow lots, were being erected around a central open area that provided air and light and a space for the children to play. But there were still land-lords who continued to make an abnormally high profit on their slum-tenement investments. Riis hit out against them hard as he kept insisting that good housing was essential to good citizenship. "A man cannot live like a pig and vote like a man."

Early in 1900, an architects' competition was held to encourage the design and building of "humane tenements that should be commercially profitable." It had been or-ganized by private concerns in cooperation with the Charity Organization Society headed by Josephine Shaw Lowell. Jacob Riis reported the competition in the February 3, 1900, issue of *Harper's Weekly.* "The tene-ment-house question," he wrote, "is the question of the health, comfort, and happiness of the vast majority of the people in modern cities." Following the competition, he announced, a Tenement-House Exhibition would be held, with a display of charts, maps, poverty and disease graphs, and tenement models. This display would later go to the Paris Exposition "to continue its work of education and of appeal to the public conscience."

In June of 1900, the Riises' older daughter Clara was married to a young doctor in the Richmond Hill Church of the Resurrection, to which the Riises belonged. Gov-ernor Roosevelt was among the guests, and many friends came from across the river to attend the reception that followed. That same summer Theodore Roosevelt was nominated for Vice President of the United States.

In addition to newspaper reporting, writing magazine articles, and lecturing, Riis was writing a book that he

called *A Ten Years' War: An Account of the Battle with
the Slum in New York*. His idea was to show the progress
that had been made in the decade since the publication of
How the Other Half Lives. He reported that after a long
fight the city had built five schools, all of them with playgrounds. (The law requiring every new school to have a
playground was a victory for Riis's almost single-handed
campaign.) He wrote glowingly of the cleaning and
paving of streets under Street Commissioner Colonel
Waring. "His broom saved more lives in the crowded
tenements than a squad of doctors. It did more; it swept
the cobwebs out of the civic brain and conscience and
set up a standard of a citizen's duty which . . . will be
ours until we have dragged other things than our pave-
ments out of the mud." He told of getting rid of the
police lodging-rooms, the stale-beer dives, and the worst
of the rear tenements. Gone were Bottle Alley, Bandits'
Roost, Thieves' Alley, and Kerosene Row. He pointed
to the opening of Mulberry Bend Park and to the building
of tenements that let in "sunshine and air and hope." He
quoted with amusement the reply of a policeman who
was asked what had become of the occupants of a torn-
down slum: "They was druv into decency, sor." With
satisfaction Riis declared, "The last four years have set us
fifty years ahead."

Riis congratulated the labor unions for "bestirring
themselves to deal with the sweatshop curse." He followed with keen interest the struggles of organized labor
to get better pay for its members and to improve their
working conditions. He had not forgotten his own early
days of manual labor. He could still remember how his

arms had ached after a day's work with hammer and saw, or cutting down trees in the forests of upper New York, or hoeing carrots in other men's gardens. All his life these memories bolstered his understanding of and sympathy with the working man. He admired Samuel Gompers' persistence and skill in bringing the trade unions together and making the American Federation of Labor a powerful force in bettering the labor situation. He agreed with Gompers that "A man's labor is not a commodity but a part of his life," and he stood behind every effort in behalf of the laboring man, so long as it was nonviolent and within the law. The improvement of living conditions played a large part, he believed, in advancing the labor movement. "Until we house our people decently," he wrote, "we cannot make them efficient workers."

That summer Jacob Riis had warnings that even his rugged constitution could not stand the hectic pace of his strenuous life. Several heart attacks, diagnosed as angina pectoris, laid him low. He rested a few weeks in the Canadian woods camp of his friend Dr. Roger Tracy, Health Department statistician, then was back in harness, working as hard as ever.

Riis was enthusiastic about Roosevelt's becoming Vice President of the United States, for he believed this good friend of his was so great that he should be on the national stage. One evening, while watching a torchlight procession in Lower Manhattan, Riis saw and heard a man perched on a truck at the lower end of the Bowery—"one of the wickedest spots in the world"—orating wildly but not very effectively in Roosevelt's behalf. Riis pushed his way through the crowd, invited himself onto the truck, and began to speak about his friendship with Roosevelt and all the things Roosevelt had accomplished as head police commissioner and as governor.

Another night during the campaign, Riis defended Roosevelt before a huge heckling audience at a People's Institute gathering at Cooper Union. Years before, this large building had been put up by Peter Cooper, a philanthropic industrialist, to provide a center for the education of working men and women. All day and every evening classes in practical subjects met here. Cooper Union was also a headquarters for laborers' civic clubs and forums. Riis, who believed strongly in education for everyone, had been one of the founders of the People's Institute, which he called a sort of "evening school in a living social science." Its purpose, he said, was "to shape a sane, informed public opinion" through public discussion and debates. Occasionally, on Sunday evenings, the Institute brought fine concerts to the hall, and more often it provided nationally known speakers. Members of the audience who disagreed with the speaker were encouraged to ask questions and air their views—a practice that often led to lively sessions.

The year 1901 was an important one for New York City, for the country, and for Jacob Riis. Once again New York citizens, spearheaded by the Citizens' Union, threw out Tammany Hall and elected a reform mayor— Seth Low, the respected President of Columbia University. Jacob Riis was one of the speakers at the Victory Dinner; his subject was "The Wage-Earning Voter." Mayor Low put into effect a new city charter that combined the various districts or boroughs of Greater New York into one political unit. He also secured money for the first municipal playground, at Seward Park, and he insisted on the enforcement of already existing laws controlling overcrowding and unsanitary conditions in tenements.

A new tenement-house commission was appointed by the state legislature, which also passed a law—the 1901 Tenement-House Act—covering slum clearance, tenement building, fire protection, light, ventilation, administration, upkeep, and inspection of tenements. This law, which was much stronger than any previous one, required that in all cities of the state with a population of more than 250,000 "all rooms and hallways be lighted and ventilated." It also imposed strict regulations regarding size of rooms, running water, fire escapes, and sanitation. It created a separate tenement-house department for New York City, with two hundred inspectors and empowered them with "ample authority." The law did not go into effect until the following year, but to no one's surprise Riis insisted on crediting it to Governor Roosevelt. Riis and his friends regarded the 1901 Tenement-House Act as a big step forward, though naturally it was bitterly attacked by speculators and small owners of slum tenements. James Ford, in his *Slums and Housing*, claimed that it brought in "a new era in tenement legislation," and he wrote: "Since the Tenement House law of 1901 it has not been possible legally to build a really bad tenement in New York." It was Jacob A. Riis, with his "highly human documents," said Mr. Ford, who was more responsible than any other for bringing about this radical law.

In the spring of 1901, Jacob and Elisabeth Riis held an open house to celebrate twenty-five years of happy married life. Scores of friends came to wish them continued happiness, and messages arrived from all over the continent and from Denmark.

On this occasion there was a special gift from the King's Daughters' Settlement on Henry Street. Ever since this organization had taken over the distribution of the "flowers for the poor" years before, Riis had been actively associated with it and its expanding activities. Now, in a ceremony conducted by Bishop Potter, the King's Daughters' Settlement formally renamed itself the Jacob A. Riis Neighborhood House. Riis was touched and pleased. In his acknowledgment speech he expressed his belief that "the world is not bad; it's good, thoroughly good. You simply have to touch it right." A little later he wrote the settlement head: "I wish I could give you more than my mere name. May the work grow in grace and usefulness. I don't care a straw if it ever grows an inch in size, so long as we fill the place in which we stand, so that . . . we may say with truth, 'I did according to my light the very best I knew how.' "

Yet for the rest of his life Riis did give this settlement house more than his name—much more. He advised and helped, contributed from his own scanty resources, and solicited funds from others. The Riis Neighborhood House did not have permanent residents; only a caretaker and his wife lived there, but each day devoted volunteers came in to conduct clubs and classes, arrange outings for children and their mothers, and do whatever they could to help the people of the neighborhood.

William McKinley and Theodore Roosevelt had won their campaign in 1900 and had been inaugurated as President and Vice President on March 4, 1901. Then, after only a few months in office, the shocking assassination of

President McKinley made Theodore Roosevelt President of the United States.

Many of Riis's acquaintances saw this as a golden opportunity for him to get for himself a fine political appointment and for them some special favor. They were disappointed that he persisted in declining any office and refused absolutely to take advantage in any way of his close friendship with the new occupant of the White House. But although he would not use his friendship to benefit himself or his friends, he did not hesitate to call Roosevelt's attention to any instance of injustice or inhumanity that came to his knowledge and that he felt the President should do something about. President Roosevelt respected Riis's knowledge and opinions. He often invited him to the White House and also to the Roosevelt home in Oyster Bay, Long Island, which was fairly accessible from Richmond Hill.

The fall of that memorable year of 1901 had been marked by the publication of the book that became the second most popular of Riis's works—after *How the Other Half Lives*. This was an informal autobiography entitled *The Making of an American*. In it Riis told of his childhood in Ribe, Denmark; of his boyhood love for Elisabeth and her rejection of him, which led to his coming to America; of his struggles in the new country and fulfilling his ambition to become a reporter; of going back to Denmark for his bride; of police reporting on Mulberry Street; of his friendship with Roosevelt; and, most of all, of his battle with the slum and his deep involvement with social and municipal reform.

The Making of an American ran serially in the *Outlook* before it was published as a book. On every page the author's vivid personality was revealed. He had no self-consciousness in writing about his happy home life and his undiminished love for his Elisabeth. He spoke with affection of his friends, exposed municipal scandals, and paid tribute to those who fought against corruption. In the breezy anecdotal style that had become his trademark he told story after story about people he had known and happenings, both humorous and pathetic, in which he had been involved. Through it all shone his everlasting optimism, his faith in mankind's innate goodness, and his great joy in living.

"It fairly bubbles over with happiness, energy, and inspiration," the *Boston Herald* said of the book, and another review mentioned its "personal charm, its buoyancy and humor and tenderness, its romance and vivid incident."

The Making of an American was an immediate success, and not only in New York. People all over the country were eager to read Riis's story for, as the *Nation* said, "His reports on slum experiences have reached an audience far beyond the City."

Riis wrote a friend happily: "In three weeks, the publisher tells me, it has run fairly out of two big editions and a third is preparing." He was even more pleased that his book had been one of five books of the year chosen to be transcribed into braille for the blind.

The popularity of *The Making of an American* made it possible for Riis to do what he had been wanting to do for several years—give up his regular newspaper job and devote himself to writing and lecturing. He figured he could still make enough for "comfortable living" for his family and for him to continue to contribute to "the work." He wrote: "I am still a young man, not far past fifty, and I have much I would do yet." This "much" was not making money or winning fame. He had no interest in doing either. It was to help make a better life for others. His undependable heart made it uncertain how much time might be left him, "But it gives me little concern," he wrote a friend; "I have got used to it." And he consoled himself with the thought that what he had might even be the "fake" kind of angina: not organic but "functional and therefore not fatal."

And so, after benefiting from the outdoor life of Dr. Tracy's Canadian camp for part of the fall of 1901, Jacob Riis said good-by to his many friends on Mulberry Street amid the usual confusion and constant interruptions in his office. He packed up his accumulation of more than twenty years of police reporting and began a different but scarcely less strenuous way of life.

13
On the Road

"It [lecturing] is very tiresome
work and yet exciting. . . . You
feel the touch with your fellows."

—Correspondence and
The Making of an American

For more than twenty years Jacob Riis worked long
hours at his newspaper crime-reporting job on Mulberry
Street, traveling to and from his office by train, ferry,
and on foot. In addition, he attended meetings of legislative commissions, of social-reform organizations, of settlement-house and civic groups, and met frequently with
social-minded individuals. When he reached home, it was
not to relax for leisurely evenings and weekends with his
family but to spend most of them writing.

He worried that he could find so little time to spend
and enjoy with his wife and children. Family outings
were rare and usually occurred on the spur of the moment. Then, with his natural high spirits, Riis always
made them occasions of great fun for the children. There
were five now. Billy, nicknamed Vivi, was the youngest.
He was born in 1894 when Ed, the oldest, was fourteen
and Kate, then the youngest, was seven. Billy naturally
became the pet of the family. Even more than the others,
Billy missed the companionship of his father. As an adult
he recalled a fishing trip his father and he took together
when he was small. He remembered it as a wonderful day

and reported that they were both "shy but affectionate." Such an outing occurred seldom, he said, because his father was usually "too busy or away."

"Away" probably meant a lecture trip. When Riis gave up his regular newspaper job in late 1901, he thought he would have more time at home. Instead, he seemed to be gone more than ever. The publication of his first book, *How the Other Half Lives,* had made him well known as "the foremost advocate of tenement-house reform in New York" and an authority on social problems. This reputation, as well as his widely reported friendship with Theodore Roosevelt, greatly increased his demand as a lecturer.

Riis thoroughly enjoyed lecturing. "No one likes talking better than I," he admitted. He had always been an easy, fluent speaker, and his audiences were fascinated by the informal way he lectured as well as by the stories of tenement life that made up so much of most of his lectures. Although these stories were often sordid, they were also dramatic, and he was skillful in balancing their grimness with touches of humor.

Perhaps the most popular of Riis's lectures was one he called "Tony and His Tribe." In this he painted an appealing picture of an undersized, undernourished, dirty and ragged slum urchin. When he first met Tony, Riis said, there was a handful of mud in the boy's fist, ready to be flung at a playmate. But when Riis held out to him a bunch of flowers, Tony dropped the mud and unbelievingly grasped the flowers. Clutching them to his bare chest so that no one could snatch them from him, he ran to the hovel where he lived with his mother and drunken father. He thrust them into an old cracked cup and there they stayed until long after they had faded. They were, Riis told his audience, perhaps the first touch of beauty that miserable place had ever seen. Thus introduced, and made more real by a few expressive slides, Tony became a living boy to Riis's listeners and his slum surroundings a matter of real concern.

Riis purposely emphasized the dark side of slum life in order to arouse the sympathy and conscience of his audience. He supported his stories with accurate facts and figures, though never to the extent of boring his listeners. "Statistics," he said, "are not my hobby. I like to get the human story out of them." And this he was a master at doing.

Riis's voice was not particularly pleasing. A local paper in a town in which he lectured compared it unkindly to "a squeaky cellar door"—a description Riis repeated with amusement. But his audiences did not seem to mind that he was not "silver-tongued," nor did they object to his Danish accent, which he never quite lost.

Magic-lantern shows were still a treat in those days before radio or television, and the appearance of a New York lecturer in a small town—or even a fair-sized one— was sure to draw a good crowd. Riis's slides, projected on a large screen, showed a side of life that most of the people who saw them had never dreamed existed. Like his stories, they touched the heart, though he always ended on a hopeful note. "We cannot get rid of tenements," he admitted, "but we can make them as nearly fit to harbor human souls as might be." Their improvement, he said, was a matter "not only of government but of humanity," and he suggested practical ways in which people could help. Then he liked to end the evening with everyone standing and singing "My Country, 'Tis of Thee."

At first Riis's speaking engagements were almost entirely in and around New York City, though as early as 1892 he had lectured in New Jersey coast towns. That summer a young author named Stephen Crane, then a correspondent for the *New York Tribune,* attended one of Riis's illustrated lectures in a New Jersey beach auditorium. He reported in his paper that the lecture was on "the unfortunates who have to stay in the crowded tenements." Crane had already written a story called "Maggie"; literary critics believe that after hearing Riis's lecture he revised it in order to describe more realistically the lives of his tenement-dwellers' characters. They also point out that Crane's Maggie closely resembles some of the real-life people described by Riis.

Lecturing anywhere—even no farther away from New York than New Jersey and New England—involved meeting all sorts of people. Jacob Riis liked this. He would talk to men and women wherever he met them and try to get their points of view, although he was not always a patient listener.

After he gave up his regular job, he was free to make longer journeys. He found traveling and lecturing less tiring than office routine. On a long train trip he could relax and watch the scenery, read, write, or make friends with the other passengers.

Early in 1902, Riis set out on a lecture tour that took him as far west as South Dakota. Later that year he made shorter tours, lecturing in New England and in New York State. He had hoped his lecture fees and the returns from his books and magazine articles would bring in enough for the "comfortable living" he coveted for his family and himself, and also enable him to do something for his settlement. To his delight he found that the money coming in was more than adequate. In addition, he was glad to have the opportunity to interest more people in contributing money for the Riis Neighborhood House activities.

A journalist reported interviewing Riis in New York's Grand Central Terminal one day as he waited for a train to take him on a lecture tour. Together they paced up and down the great concourse, talking. As Riis warmed up to his theme, the reporter said, his face flushed and "he told me a great many vital things in his intense, rapid, tumbling Scandinavian English." One of Riis's comments the interviewer passed on to his readers was: "Many of these poor people who have committed crimes are victims of birth and environment. They are choked by filth and greed; they struggle, get blinded, and then something unfortunate happens." When the journalist asked what he and others could do to help, Riis suggested studying the needs of young men who line up on street corners. He also advised working in a settlement house or downtown church, and ended, "Be neighborly; get to work."

Riis's major concern in social betterment naturally was centered in the New York slums he knew so well, but he was also acquainted with conditions in other American cities. He had a firsthand familiarity with the poorest parts of Chicago, where Jane Addams's work at Hull House was an inspiration to him, and with the slums of Washington, Pittsburgh, St. Louis, and Boston. His diaries for 1904 through 1906 show that he lectured in practically

The Mulberry Bend

Left: Minding the baby
—a scene in Gotham
Court

Below: Girl and baby on
doorstep

Above: On the roof of the Barracks

Right: In the home of an Italian ragpicker, Jersey Street

Below: Jersey Street tenements

Above: Necktie workshop in a Division Street tenement
Below: East Side Public School (Allen or Chrystie Street)

Above: Vegetable stand in "the Bend". *Below:* Old house on a Bleecker Street back lot, between Mercer and Greene Streets

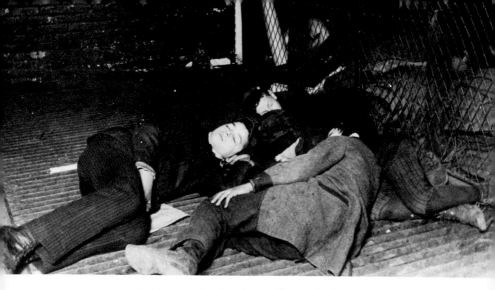

Above: 3:00 A.M. in the *Sun* office. *Below:* "Five cents a spot"—lodgers in a crowded Bayard Street tenement

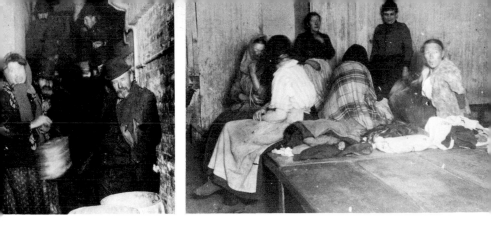

Left: Police station lodgers waiting to be let out. *Right:* Women in Elizabeth Street Police Station lodging room

Above: In a 7-cent lodging house. *Below:* Street Arabs, barelegged in Mulberry Street

Above: Tenement-house yard

Left: Rushing the growler (pail of beer)

Below: An old rear tenement in Roosevelt Street

all the large cities of the country, including San Francisco and Los Angeles in the West and New Orleans and Dallas in the South. Wherever he was, he made his lecture not merely the story of New York's problems and progress but took pains to make it of practical value to the community he was in. Often he would arrive early enough to visit the city's poorest district before his lecture so that he could speak with some authority on the local situation. He was gratified to have it said that he was awakening the social conscience all over America through his lectures and his writings. Year by year the number of Riis's listeners grew; so did their responsiveness to his message.

As Riis's reputation became nationwide, large lecture bureaus like Redpath, Lyceum, and Chautauqua were glad to "handle" him. Earlier, when he had made his own lecture arrangements, he had underestimated himself and set his fee too low. The lecture bureaus charged sometimes as high as one hundred and fifty dollars and took care of all the details of hiring a hall, travel, hotels, and publicity. But they booked him in places a long way from home; this sometimes necessitated his being away from his family and his New York activities for weeks at a time.

On his long journeys Riis sent his wife and children lengthy, lively letters written on trains and in hotels. Sometimes he suggested: "Get out your map and follow along." Billy, the youngest son, who was away at school, said that his father's letters to him were read aloud in the geography class.

Riis also wrote often to the staff at the Neighborhood House. At least once, and probably oftener, he composed an appeal-for-funds letter to be typed and sent out from the settlement to certain private schools. He wrote, too, to friends and to leaders in the social-reform movement, not only in New York but in other cities—letters full of interest in their activities, inquiries about experimental methods, and suggestions of his own for practical imaginative new programs.

In January, 1903, Riis delivered a series of three lectures at a divinity school in Philadelphia. These were later made available in book form under the title *The Peril and Preservation of the Home.* His main point in this series was the need to strengthen the home, "the key to good citizenship . . . on which it all hinges." Eighty percent of the crime in cities, he quoted a prison-association secretary as saying, comes from those "whose homes had ceased to be sufficiently separate, decent, and desirable to afford what are regarded as ordinary wholesome influences of home and family." The marvel, said Riis, "was not that children from overcrowded, dirty homes grew up to be diseased, drunkards, and criminals, but that so many of them, in spite of their early surroundings, grew up to be decent, self-respecting men and women."

After one of these Philadelphia lectures Riis was seized with one of his dreaded heart attacks while walking on the street with a friend. "I had great difficulty in getting him to the train and into his sleeping berth," his friend wrote. Yet this did not keep Riis from leaving almost immediately for a lengthy lecture tour of the Midwest. "The time goes and so far I am all right," he wrote his Philadelphia friend, although he admitted, "I was more than half dead that night." He added, "The very hardest trip on my list I have cut out; the others I tackle and shall get through with all right, please God." And from a small town in Iowa he wrote later, "I am getting along much better; now for over a week without any trouble at all!"

Whenever his lecture tours permitted and he could manage it, Riis stopped off at Washington to call at the White House. President Theodore Roosevelt continued to be for him the ideal citizen, the nearly perfect man. Theirs was the great friendship of his life, as rare and beautiful an experience in its way as was his lifelong love for Elisabeth. Nor had becoming President in any way diminished Roosevelt's affection for Riis. He expressed this affection in many personal acts of thoughtfulness which showed that he truly felt, as he later said, "Jake" to be "one of my truest and closest friends" and "like my own brother." When Riis, breakfasting at the White House with the President and his wife, mentioned his concern over the illness of his mother in Denmark, the President and Mrs. Roosevelt sent her a cable wishing her a return to health. They arranged to have Billy Riis pay a visit to the White House and gave him a wonderful time. And when the Riis Neighborhood House opened its gym, the President sent a telegram of congratulation and Mrs. Roosevelt sent flowers from the White House gardens.

Riis reached home from his 1903 spring lecture tour "so tired that I absolutely shun mankind . . . but the garden and summer weather will soon restore me, please God." His heart, he writes, had not troubled him for months. "Still, I am prepared for an ambush in that quarter, always." It was when he became overexcited or out of breath, he said, that he was uncomfortably conscious of his heart.

That summer Riis visited the boys' reformatory on Randall's Island in the East River and wrote a magazine

article about it. He reported what the boys had told him
—that they were hungry and unhappy. He added that
they were not decently clothed and that, mixed in with
thieves, the bad were corrupting the good. The old reformatory, he said, should be torn down and replaced by
a farm school farther away from the city, where the boys
would learn to become good and useful citizens. Then
Randall's Island should be made into a municipal park.

During this summer at home Riis revised his *Out of
Mulberry Street* collection of stories, renaming it *Children
of the Tenements*. In his preface he said the stories "grew
out of my work as police reporter for nearly a quarter of
a century." Most of the forty stories had first been published in the *Sun* or in various magazines.

In August, Riis wrote in his neglected diary: "Spent
yesterday with the President, had a lovely day." And he
added that he was going to write a book about him. "It
will not be a 'life'—that is far too big for me; just my own
impressions of a beloved friend." Roosevelt, after serving
out McKinley's unfinished term, had decided to seek the
presidency on his own, and his friend "Jake" wanted to
do everything in his power, even to writing a book, to
help him win the election.

By the time Riis began his lecture tours again in the
fall, his Roosevelt book was beginning to come out
serially in the *Outlook*. That fall Tammany came back
into power, following Seth Low's two-year reform administration. The Tammany methods were more subtle
now than in the old days; the Tammany bosses knew they
were being watched by men like Riis and by civic groups
like the newly formed Women's Municipal League. Besides writing against the Tammany abuses Riis frequently

spoke to gatherings of civic organizations, at the Y.M.C.A., at schools and settlement houses. But as his lecture tours became lengthier, he had less and less time for informal speechmaking. "My work," he wrote, "takes me traveling a great deal from October to June."

In December, Riis went to Washington to speak to a Senate and House joint committee on housing for the poor of the District of Columbia. Before his appearance he made a tour of the District's slum area. He made his remarks considerably more personal by his mention of seeing Senate barbershop towels hanging on a line in one of the slum backyards. His talk bore fruit; a short time after his appearance a housing company was appointed to build some "cheap but healthful dwellings" for Washington's poor.

"Come now, New Year," Riis wrote in his new diary on January 1, 1904, "and let's see how we can get on together. If you'll behave I will. But I warn you no tricks!"

That spring, while Riis was on a lecture tour in several midwestern states, *Theodore Roosevelt, the Citizen* came out in book form. Its purpose, Riis stated, was not just to boom Roosevelt for the presidency, but to tell of him as "the friend, the man." He dedicated the book "To the Young Men of America," and held Roosevelt up to them as a man for whom "honor goes before profit," a man who believed men can be trusted if you believe in the good in them; a man who emphasized the importance of work and the "gospel of will." For nothing is more certain, said Riis, revealing his own philosophy, than "what a man wills himself to be, that he will be."

The Riises spent the summer of 1904 in Denmark, returning well before the presidential election in November.

Right after it Riis set out on a lengthy lecture tour. In reply to a friend's letter asking him about his reactions to Roosevelt's becoming President, Riis wrote: "Did I rejoice in Roosevelt's election? Well, rather! And yet I didn't throw up my hat as I thought I would have done. It was too big a blessing for that. I felt a bit awed by it. But that night I slept as I have not done in years, and I went west feeling as if my life had suddenly come to full fruit. It was a blessed, peaceful happiness. I was glad and I felt that the whole land lay in the sunlight of happiness."

This tour took Riis farther west than he had been before. Seeing his country was, he said, "a liberal and a great education." He regretted the fog in California, the incessant rain in Washington and Oregon, and especially having to spend the holidays far from his family. But he reported happily that he had had no trouble with his heart.

In the mountains Riis acted like a boy. He bragged, "Threw my first snowball this winter among the peaks of Sierra——Mtns." And his friend Rabbi Stephen Wise, who was with him when he saw Mt. Hood for the first time said that, in his pleasure and excitement Riis had "tears in his eyes, then jumped about like a child."

In Montana, Riis and a friend rode horseback into the mountains where they cooked bacon and coffee and climbed a peak. On the way down they encountered an old miner living in a clay-roofed shack. He turned out to be of Danish blood and he brought out a carefully preserved year-old Danish newspaper, which prompted Riis to make a second trip up this mountain to take the old man a package of food and books. And before he left Helena, Riis made his friends there promise to keep an eye on the old Danish miner and see that he came to no harm.

Of course Riis returned to the East in time to attend the Roosevelt inauguration in Washington on the fourth of March. He felt, he said, a satisfaction and a "great peace." Then he went out to Ohio to lecture, down to North Carolina, and up into New England. Everywhere his lectures were drawing crowds. Checks, and sometimes gifts—like the box of Wenatchee apples from the Northwest—went to the Riis Neighborhood House. Riis was happy to be telling the people of America of the problems and potentials of "the other half." As for himself, he said delightedly that he had now saved thirty thousand dollars —almost enough to retire on!

14

"Denmark
I Love, but
America Is Home"

"America is my land after all."
—Ware, *Jacob A. Riis*

Frequent letters to and from the family and friends in Denmark kept the Riises in touch with what was going on in their native land. The Richmond Hill home was still pretty much a Danish-American one, although Jacob Riis encouraged his children in every way to grow up to be true Americans. Good citizenship was a principle he both preached and practiced. In his opinion this included —but did not end with—personal integrity, respect for law, responsibility in voting, and an effort to get better laws passed and then enforced with justice to all.

It was eighteen years after his first trip back to Denmark in 1875 to marry his sweetheart before Riis returned. When, in 1893, he finally was financially able to go back with his family, it was a sentimental journey. His father and mother were still living, though he was shocked to see how much his father had aged. It was strange too to find his little sister Sophie grown into a young lady and his foster sister Emma middle-aged like himself. He was glad his parents were having this chance to see his children and the children the opportunity to get acquainted with their grandparents. There was a close bond between Riis and his father, and Jacob was touched by the old man's pride in having a son who was a writer.

In the quaint little town of his childhood Riis walked along the narrow, crooked streets and looked up at the storks' nests perched beside the tall chimneys on the tile-roofed houses. What a contrast to Mulberry Bend! Growing up in Ribe, he decided, undoubtedly had much to do with his hatred of city slums and his conviction that a good environment was essential to a good life.

Four years later, when Clara was seventeen, she went to Denmark and stayed several months. In 1899, Riis again returned, this time alone, to visit his mother, who had become a widow. On his way he stopped in London. He wandered about its slum area, finding it bleak and depressing and without the hopeful air he felt in New York. He stopped in Holland, too, but most of his time was spent in Denmark.

One purpose of this trip was to get some ideas for magazine articles. With this in mind Riis sat on the Ribe "gossip benches" where old men smoked their pipes and talked about the "good old days." He lingered in the ancient Domkirke, recalling the day he and Elisabeth were married there and the Christmas Eve candlelight services he had gone to as a child. How well he remembered the solemn pealing of the great bells! He wandered outside the little town and sat beside the brook where he and his boyhood companions had caught sunfish, built bonfires, and roasted potatoes and the fish they had caught. He walked across the moors and into the forests of moss-grown beeches and gnarled oaks.

In Copenhagen it had been arranged for Riis to be formally presented to King Christian. A courtier instructed him in the proper way to make his approach. But, said Riis, "I saw a tired and lonely old man, to whom my heart went out on the instant, and I went right up and shook hands and told him how much I thought of him."

The King commented on the little silver cross Riis was wearing in his lapel. Riis took it off and offered it to the King, explaining that it was the King's Daughters' emblem. He told of their distributing flowers to the poor and then establishing a settlement house so they could be of more help to the needy. The King would not take the pin, but after Riis's return to America a small box arrived from Copenhagen. It was from King Christian and it contained the coveted gold Cross of Dannebrog—the old crusaders' cross, the Danish medal of honor. It became Riis's most precious possession.

He wore it one evening years later when he and his wife were invited to a formal dinner at the White House. Mrs. Riis wore her silver-anniversary dress and the thought crossed Riis's mind as the President escorted her in to dinner that if her parents could have seen her then, they might not think she had done so badly after all in marrying the son of a poor schoolmaster! But he felt embarrassed that he had worn the Dannebrog Cross because none of the other guests was wearing a decoration. The President, somehow sensing his friend's feeling, took him aside and told him he was "honored and touched" to have the distinguished Danish decoration grace the White House table. Immediately all was well and Riis again became his exuberant self.

"Denmark I Love, but America Is Home"

Toward the end of Riis's 1899 stay in Denmark he had gone to Elsinore, where his mother had grown up. There he had come down with a serious attack of malaria that put him to bed for several weeks. From his bed he could look out on the sea. One day, as he was recovering, he saw a ship sailing by flying the American flag. "I sat up in bed and shouted, laughed and cried by turns," he confessed. "I knew then that it was my flag; that my children's home was mine indeed; that I also had become an American in truth. And I thanked God and . . . went home, healed."

The American flag had great emotional appeal for Jacob Riis. The Danish and the American flags, he wrote, stand "side by side in my affection." He remembered that "I was a big boy when I first saw in the harbor of Copenhagen the one other flag [than the Danish] that gripped my imagination in the same way. It blew straight out from the peak of an American ship, and it seemed to me, if anything, more beautiful." He called the Stars and Stripes "the flag of my home, of my manhood's years and of my pride." To "the red and white of my father's flag," he said, "I added only the blue of heaven, where wrongs are righted."

Riis's first magazine article about Denmark had appeared in *Century Magazine* in 1896. In it he described a winter storm and shipwreck on the bleak North Sea. "Long winter nights," he wrote, "when the west wind tore at our bedroom window and howled about the gables, we lay awake listening for the voice of the bell in the old gray tower of the Domkirke. When the storm shook the tower to the foundations, the big bell gave forth a moan, then sobbed through the night, filling it with a nameless dread. We children pulled the bedclothes over our heads when we heard it above the smashing of roof tiles on the cobblestones and the watchman's warning cry that the sea was 'coming in' and tried to think of the prayer for those 'in danger of the deep.' "

Perhaps it was this story that prompted Riis's friend Richard Gilder, editor of the *Century Magazine,* to suggest Riis do more pieces with a Danish background. On that 1899 summer trip Riis did gather many ideas for articles. The first one was about "Hamlet's Castle" in the town of Elsinore, where he had been so ill. Others—some of them not written until several years later—were based on childhood recollections, and several told the stories of little-known Danish heroes of olden times.

In the summer of 1904, with no regular newspaper job to hold him down and with the increased income from his writing and lectures, Riis again took the whole family to Denmark. His mother had died the previous year and Riis's foster sister Emma was now head of the household. There was a special reason for going back that summer, for the ancient Domkirke had been restored and was to be rededicated by King Christian himself. The little town was thrilled at the thought of the King's coming to Ribe for the ceremonies. So were the Riises—the children to see a real king, and their parents to see at close hand the revered head of their native land.

Following the impressive dedication ceremonies in the Domkirke there was a festive banquet, which Jacob Riis attended. During the dinner a message came to the table at which he was seated. It was from King Christian, announcing that he was about to drink to the health of Jacob Riis.

"I was never so proud in all my days," Riis said. It was especially pleasant, he confessed, to be honored before townspeople who had looked askance at him as a youth because he "did not do according to the rules but broke over the traces every way and went off to America."

Riis visited the graves of his parents and brothers. At the Old People's Home he chatted with a childhood nurse, with an old man who had played the fiddle at dancing school when Riis was a boy, and with a woman who had come once or twice a month to his home to collect soiled clothes and to wash them, along with "four or five women beating clothes with wooden mallets knee deep in the creek." He talked to the pupils at the little school, telling them about his friendship with the American President. He attended a wedding at which the bride, a friend's daughter, was crowned with the traditional myrtle wreath.

While the family was in Copenhagen, Mr. and Mrs. Riis were invited to dine with the Crown Prince and Princess at their palace of Charlottenborg, not far from the city. They drove out with the American minister to Denmark and his wife. Riis was formally dressed, wearing a borrowed top hat and the Dannebrog Cross sent him by King Christian. But they found the occasion informal and their host and hostess friendly and unaffected. After the midday dinner the royal couple and their American guests strolled in the gardens, conversing about many things, including America and the contribution made to it by the Danes who lived there.

Altogether the summer was a great success. In an article published a few months later in the *Outlook* and titled

"Our Beautiful Summer," Riis called the trip "one long holiday without a cloud."

While in Denmark, Riis brought himself up to date on social developments in the small country. This was not difficult, for through the years he had kept himself well informed on what went on in the way of social reforms in Denmark—as indeed he did on those in other countries. He was proud of the progressiveness of his native land. Being a small agricultural country, its social problems were naturally different from those of a huge industrial nation, yet Riis believed some of Denmark's ideas and methods would work well in America.

There was, for example, the Danish custom of sending a "Good Works" card instead of flowers to a family in which there had been a death. The card stated that its sender was making a contribution to some charity in memory of the deceased. Riis thought of the large amounts of money spent in America for funeral flowers and how it could buy food and other necessities for the poor. Why couldn't the United States adopt this sensible "Good Works" plan? And so he wrote a description of it in the *Sun,* headed: "Flowers for the Dead to be Replaced by Kind Deeds to the Living." The plan, he wrote, was in use not only in Denmark but also in Sweden, England, France, and Austria. At the time the idea did not seem to appeal to many Americans, though there were some favorable reactions to the article. Years later, however, many thoughtful persons adopted this Danish custom.

Riis also called the attention of Americans to Copenhagen's "Tag Day" when "Help the Children" contributions were solicited. And he described and recommended the Danes' "Lucky Penny" custom. Every father of a

126

newborn child received from the Association for Denmark's Blind a "lucky penny," together with a money-order blank and a note suggesting that the new father acknowledge his "lucky penny" by making a donation to the needy blind as "a gift from one who sees the light for the first time to those who will never see it." In his description of this plan in the *Outlook*, Riis said Sweden and Norway were adopting it and "all Europe wants to know about it. Has it no significance for the friends of the needy blind in our country?" It did not seem to have.

One Danish idea Jacob Riis wrote about did catch on, at first slowly and then with increasing speed. In "The Christmas Stamp" in the July 6, 1907, *Outlook*, he told of a special stamp sold and used in Denmark at the holiday season. Its purpose was not to carry mail but to build hospitals for children with tuberculosis. A Danish postal official had suggested it, and papers and posters all over Denmark had promoted the idea. Between two and four million stamps had been used the first year, more the second, and in the third year nearly four times as many. The sale, said Riis, "surpassed their wildest dreams."

Why shouldn't the United States, too, have a Christmas stamp to help fight tuberculosis? Riis asked. Its printing could be handled by an antituberculosis committee, its promotion by educational media, and its sale by the government. Riis mentioned that the National Association for the Study and Prevention of Tuberculosis, recently organized in New York, already had fourteen hundred members but needed funds. What better way to raise them than by adopting Denmark's idea of a Christmas stamp?

No one in New York took up the challenge, but in

Wilmington, Delaware, Emily P. Bissell, secretary of the Delaware branch of the American Red Cross, acted on Riis's suggestion. Through her efforts and the cooperation of a Philadelphia newspaper a stamp designed that same year brought in several thousand dollars for the anti-tuberculosis cause in the Wilmington-Philadelphia area. The idea spread. In 1908, the American Red Cross took over the sale of the Red Cross Christmas seals, as they began to be called, and in the first three years realized nearly a million dollars with which to fight tuberculosis. Two years later the National Tuberculosis Association joined the American Red Cross in sponsoring the little Christmas seal, and from 1920 on assumed sole responsibility for it. It has been, said the *New York Times* in 1949, when crediting the idea to Jacob Riis, "the chief factor in arousing the public to the possibility of the ultimate conquest of this disease which then was foremost among death-dealers."

Jacob Riis's personal interest in fighting tuberculosis was due not only to the fact that it was this disease which had killed his brothers, but to the suffering he saw it causing in the overcrowded tenements of New York. Elated by the success of the Christmas seal, he wrote, "All over the world the little stamps have become bullets in the war on the White Plague which humanity is at last in the way of winning."

Jacob Riis loved new ideas—his own or anyone else's, American or Danish. He never claimed others' ideas as his own, but neither did he hesitate to use them if they could help in wiping out evils, righting wrongs, or solving difficulties. And he wrote with deep sincerity: "I . . . thank God that he sent me over the sea to cast in my lot with a country and with a people that do not everlastingly follow worm-eaten precedent, but are young enough and strong enough and daring enough to make it when need be."

15

"A Blast of Cheer"

"It is great to have lived in a day
that sees such things done."

—*The Battle with the Slum*

During the few months that Theodore Roosevelt was Vice President of the United States, before the assassination of William McKinley made him President, he addressed the National Conference of Charities. Of course it was his friend "Jake" who had asked him to speak at this gathering of social workers from all over the country. In his address on "Reform through Social Work," the Vice President paid tribute to Jacob Riis, calling him "the most useful citizen of New York." Riis, he said, knew, probably better than any other man, "the needs of the varied people who make up the great bulk of New York's population." Besides his earnestness and zeal Riis had, said Roosevelt, "the great gift of making others see what he saw and feel what he felt." Riis, he added, "works as well as talks . . . and he has high courage, a disinterested desire to do good, and a sane, wholesome common sense, as well as a sense of humor."

Jacob Riis, also a speaker at that national conference of social workers, demonstrated the courage, common sense, and humor Roosevelt attributed to him by daring to call his address "A Blast of Cheer," introducing this note of joy into the convention's weighty discussions of social problems. "I would blow a blast of cheer on my bugle and when you know that it comes from the police reporter's office in Mulberry Street, where the outlook is always grim, then you may know that it is an honest blast." If the dawn could be seen there, Riis told these social workers from all over the country, then "it is bright enough for all the world to make out."

The problems were much the same everywhere, Riis said, and everywhere the need was for "not charity, but justice." Poverty, he said, was "the evidence of a maladjusted society." The more firmly it was entrenched, the harder it was to root out. "Prevention is the true cure. . . . The way to fight the slum is to head it off."

To many people brought up in the earlier belief that poverty was a fact of life (for others, of course, not for themselves) this talk of prevention came as a rather startling idea. They found it hard to believe that private charity was no longer an acceptable means of dealing with poverty, or to accept the theory that environment was responsible for most of the miseries of the poor and that society was responsible for that environment. Yet they had to admit that disease, death, and crime rates had dropped with the building of better tenements. Much earlier, said Riis, a tenement-house commission had discovered that the trouble was not with the people but with their surroundings and had reported: "The people are all right, if we only give them half a chance."

Riis was continually emphasizing the underlying good in people. He told the assembled social workers several stories from his experience as police reporter. One was of "the Kid," a "delinquent" who broke away from the police as they were taking him to jail and risked his life to rescue a baby from under the wheels of a runaway street-car. Another was of a tough young girl, called with reason Fighting Mary, who at a settlement-house Thanksgiving dinner lovingly stroked her piece of mince pie—the first she had ever seen—and put it in her pocket to take to her mother. Still another story was of the wife whose drunken husband beat her cruelly but who, when he died, spent every cent of her insurance money to buy a fine funeral for him.

Try to understand these people! Riis implored his social-worker listeners. Appeal to the good in them! Have faith in them! Use heart, not just laboratory methods, in dealing with them. Remember that "the slum is the problem not only of government but of humanity." And don't be discouraged—"the light comes as we work toward it."

Two years after *A Ten Years' War* was published, Riis brought the record up to date in a revision he called *The Battle with the Slum*.

In this book he stated: "Not in the thirty years before did we advance as in these three, though Tammany blocked the way most of the time. It is great to have lived in a day that sees such things done." And he went on in *The Battle with the Slum* to tell about the building of new schools, the opening of kindergartens, and the construction of what he calls, not braggingly but with real truth, "my" small parks. As these parks appeared, he says, the police remarked that "the gangs vanished as if by magic." He mentions the public baths opened by the city; their popularity proves, he says, that the "great unwashed" were not dirty from choice!

The play piers described in *The Battle with the Slum* were an innovation Riis and others had thought up. The city called them roof gardens, because they were set up on the roofs of the piers that extended into the East River. After the success of the first one, opened in 1897, several more were built—"great, handsome structures," said Riis, and quiet, since "the street is far away with its noise."

Of the opening of one of them he wrote: "Half the East Side swarmed over . . . with shrieks of delight, and carried the mayor and the city government, who had come to see the show, fairly off their feet." These play piers, he said, were used by "waifs and 'little mothers' often scarcely larger than the young siblings it was their duty to 'mind'; and under the guidance of matron and kindergarten teacher learned new ways of delight, good manners and cleanliness. Here in the evening thronged the parents and young lovers, out of the tenement furnaces into the cool of the river night, to listen to the band and 'walk around the pier in a constantly moving procession.' "

Decent housing was still, in Riis's mind, the one thing more important than play areas and good schools. The early years of the twentieth century saw great advances in tenement-house construction. Riis greatly admired Alfred T. White, one of the pioneers in this field. This Brooklyn architect designed and built sound, sanitary tenements that could be rented reasonably and yet at a profit to the owners. "Humane tenements that should be commercially profitable" were also being put up by others. The Association for the Improvement of the Poor raised a million dollars to erect well-built fireproof tenements with adequate light and air. The tenants for them,

selected for "steadiness, sobriety, cleanliness," appreciated
the sensible, friendly management of these buildings.

Another development Riis mentioned with approval in
The Battle with the Slum was the building of several
hotels for men—poor men. Named Mills Hotels after the
philanthropic banker who financed them, they very
nearly put out of business the dirty lodging houses a
police inspector called "nurseries of crime." The Mills
Hotels were a boon to young country lads stranded in the
city and to lonely older men. Inexpensive but not free,
they helped a man keep his self-respect by making him
pay his way.

Riis hoped that better transportation, new bridges, and
the extension of streetcar lines would induce more people
to live outside the city and commute to work, as he had
done for so many years. Lower land values away from
the crowded city areas would make it possible for them
to build small homes. To Riis even the best tenement
home was not as desirable for a family as a house. "Man
is not made to be forced to live all his life in a box, packed
away with his fellows like so many herring in a barrel."
But suburban living was popular only with the better-paid
workers; the very poor still wanted to live near their
work and their relatives and friends. How they could
prefer "the rush and roar of the city" to "grass and trees
and birds and the salt breath of the sea" was something
Riis could not understand. For himself, he felt he must
live "where there are trees and birds and green hills and
where the sky is blue above." He was sorry when a Jewish
philanthropist who bought land in southern New Jersey
on which to resettle Jewish immigrants could find comparatively few who wanted to leave New York.

134

By the early nineteen hundreds many organizations and agencies had been set up to help improve the condition of the poor. A few had been in existence longer, among them the Children's Aid Society. As far back as 1894 Riis had written enthusiastically of its work. Even then it had maintained industrial and night schools, a farm school, and day schools for over five thousand children who were too dirty or ragged or non-English-speaking to be welcome in the public schools. It ran one lodging house for girls and five for boys, many of whom had been driven out of their tenement homes by brutality or drunkenness. It was also saving thousands of youngsters from the "hopeless corruption of the slum" by placing them with families in Midwestern villages and on farms. "The cost of sending one homeless child to a western home is twenty-five dollars," Riis ended his September, 1894, *Forum* article, and he gave the address of the Society and the name of the treasurer. Years later, in *A Ten Years' War*, Riis again mentions the Children's Aid Society, congratulating it on its forty-six years of useful service.

The Society for the Prevention of Cruelty to Children was established to look after the needs of children younger than those cared for by the Children's Aid Society. Riis recalled the pitiful scene that had brought about its founding. Little Mary Ellen had been so badly beaten by her parents that she could not walk and was carried into police court in a horse blanket. The judge wanted to send her to a hospital to be cared for but had no authority to do so, since legally parents had all rights over their children. Then he had an idea. He invoked for Mary Ellen "a dog's right"—a term often used by the Society for the Prevention of Cruelty to Animals. Riis

135

said that grown men in the court wept at the sight of poor battered Mary Ellen and at the judge's having to resort to "a dog's right" to get human treatment for her. Not only did this incident result in the founding of the Society for the Prevention of Cruelty to Children; it was also responsible for a law that protected a human child from abuse by anyone, including parents.

Riis often referred to himself as a "loner." "I am not good in the ranks," he said. Yet any agency working actively and intelligently for the betterment of "the other half" could count on his hearty support. He was involved with most of the settlement houses, especially with the College Settlement where Dr. Jane E. Robbins was located, the Henry Street Settlement that Lillian Wald had founded, and the King's Daughters' Settlement, particularly after it became the Jacob A. Riis Neighborhood House. They could all count on Riis's support in their campaigns to improve housing, correct bad factory and sweatshop practices, and to protect children. He never hesitated to criticize or to congratulate, and he continually urged his settlement-house friends to keep their activities on a practical, common-sense, down-to-earth basis. Neighborliness was still the keynote, not cold scientific experiments or vague social theories. He had, Riis said, "no stomach for abstract discussions of social wrongs. . . . A human being in misery is not a bug to be stuck upon a pin for leisurely investigation and learned indexing."

In *The Battle with the Slum* Riis wrote: "When I look back . . . it does seem as if we had come a good way, and as if all the turmoil and the bruises and the fighting had been worthwhile." Worthwhile indeed! And most of the lengthy list of social reforms could be traced directly or indirectly to Jacob Riis. In August, 1903, the popular *McCall's Magazine* ran a long article by Lincoln Steffens about his friend Riis. In it Steffens said, "No citizen of New York ever devoted himself so completely to the welfare of the city as Riis, and truly no one has accomplished so many specific tangible reforms."

Riis was feeling very happy about all the progress toward social justice being made not only in New York but all over America when suddenly he suffered the severest blow of his life. In May, 1905, after a few weeks of illness, his boyhood sweetheart and faithful wife of many years died. As, helpless, he watched her struggle against bronchial pneumonia, "I have thrown up all my lecturing and given notice that my place is here by her bedside," Riis wrote. "I am conscience-stricken that while I was traveling and lecturing she has been lonesome and longing for me. God help us, we have not so many years left that we can afford to waste a day away from one another."

He sent for both the older sons. Ed had married and was working on a newspaper in California and John was in Denver. Clara, too, returned. Eighteen-year-old Kate and eleven-year-old Billy (Vivi) were still at home. Telegrams, letters, messages, and flowers poured in from all over the country, including, of course, the White House.

After her death, Jacob Riis, grief-stricken, lost and lonely, tried to fill his days with work. His friends were a great support and help. In June he spent a few days at the home of Dr. Robbins in Wethersfield, Connecticut, where Kate and Billy had visited earlier. In July he traveled to Oyster Bay for an overnight visit with the

President and the next month accompanied him on a trip to Virginia. He went to Greenwich, Connecticut, to have dinner with Mrs. Lowell, whose health was failing, and he spent two weeks with friends in the Adirondacks. This outdoor experience did him good, both physically and mentally. So did a few weeks spent at the familiar Canadian camp of his friend Dr. Tracy, where he took Vivi—"a lonely little fellow."

But Jacob Riis was not one to sit long on the sidelines, no matter what his personal feelings. In the fall he felt the urge to be part of the action again—part of the movement toward a better world that he optimistically believed to be "constant, irresistible." He resumed his activities in organizations and on committees, and in October declared himself ready to start out on another lecture tour. To a friend he wrote: "Now my work begins, and perhaps I shall find in it the peace that has not come to me yet."

16

Another Go at It

"The man who believes in the
world growing better helps make
it better."

—*Theodore Roosevelt, the Citizen*

The motto of the Jacob A. Riis Neighborhood House was
"For all God's children," and it aimed "at making a real
brotherhood on earth." The settlement house was open
without distinction to children and their parents of every
race and creed. Here Italians and Irish, East Europeans
and Negroes, Scandinavians and Chinese, Jews, Catholics,
and Protestants met on equal terms. Here the holidays of
different countries and religions were celebrated by all.

The Neighborhood House meant more to Riis every
year. He gave to it time, thoughtful effort, and money.
Some of his lecture fees went toward paying off the
mortgage on the house next door, which had been
bought to double the capacity and opportunities of the
settlement. He also interested many wealthy people in
contributing checks. Ten private schools, inspired by his
lectures, pledged their help toward the support of the
settlement. But when the boys in one school failed to
meet their pledge and their headmaster sent in his personal check to cover it, Riis, with his usual insistence on
fairness, had the check returned to him. Many small un-

solicited contributions came to Riis from individuals who wanted to help. These he was scrupulously careful to acknowledge and to put where he felt they would do the most good.

Jacob Riis never had any ambition to make money. "I do not wish to be rich," he wrote his foster sister Emma, "and it is just as well because I never will be, thank Heaven. I do not have time to save." He spent little on himself, though all his life he was generous with others. Besides the settlement, his family still accounted for a large share of his expenditures. Clara's marriage had not turned out well, and her father sent money to her and her children. Billy was at boarding school, and Kate was a boarder in a Richmond Hill neighbor's home. Two years later, when she was twenty, she married a promising young surgeon whom she had met on shipboard when the family had gone to Denmark; the couple went to live in Minnesota.

Riis's heart problem increased. In 1905, while on a lecture tour in California, he had to spend three weeks at a Santa Barbara sanitarium. Early the next year he was twice "laid away for a while to tame a rebellious heart" in a New York hospital. But he soon was out lecturing again, exclaiming, "Let us wear out if we must, never rust." After still another attack and many occasional "fits of pain," he reluctantly admitted it was time he started getting his heart repaired. He spent part of the summer at the Canadian camp he loved, and the Christmas holidays at a sanitarium in Michigan. But he could not lose the habit of pushing himself. Even when complete rest was prescribed, he insisted on writing, both magazine articles and innumerable letters to promote various civic and social reforms and to bring in money for the constantly expanding work of the Riis Neighborhood House. The mortgage that hung over it worried him, and he was tremendously relieved when this was paid off at the end of 1905.

Jacob Riis was essentially a "home" type of man. In a letter to Emma he admits, "I am no good alone." Two years after his first wife's death he asked his friends at the Neighborhood House to rejoice with him that he would soon "no longer be a homeless wanderer on earth." He was going to "make Miss Mary Phillips my wife and give my little boy a mother and a home. Miss Phillips has been for two years my secretary and right hand, and she loves my boy. He loves her back. . . . I think that I shall be able to do my work better for the companionship of a strong, loving, and gentle woman."

Mary Phillips, twenty-five years Jacob Riis's junior, had been a St. Louis socialite and had been educated abroad. Because of her interest in social work she had, as Riis wrote, become his secretary shortly after his wife's death. After their marriage, the Richmond Hill home, which had been rented, was re-established and again became the center of Riis's life and, during boarding-school vacations, a home for the thirteen-year-old son.

It was a happy marriage for both husband and wife. Jacob Riis appreciated his "clever, understanding, and dear wife," and Mary Riis, at first impressed with her husband's accomplishments and his fine qualities, grew to love him devotedly. She helped him with his writing, with his correspondence, and with his work for the

141

settlement. She became a second mother to Vivi and a real homemaker and hostess in the now more American than Danish Richmond Hill home.

Riis's continuing feeling of financial responsibility, both to the settlement and to his family, kept him on the lecture platform. He was also influenced by the habit of years, by a restless energy, and by his genuine enjoyment of the work. He had, too, a driving desire to go on contributing his bit toward social betterment and toward encouraging others to do the same. The lecture bureaus urged him to continue. They had no difficulty in getting speaking engagements for the man who was considered a leading authority on American social problems, who was an entertaining, informative, and inspiring speaker, and who was, besides, a close friend of Theodore Roosevelt.

Riis's lectures did not change much with the years. He still talked a good deal about early days in the New York slums, contrasting them with present conditions. He compared the current practices with the old-time handouts—the doling out of alms, which made the giver feel good, but which often encouraged pauperism and begging. He said that when he was young he, too, had indulged in private charity. Every night as he passed an old crone sitting on a bench rocking her baby he used to drop a nickel into her outstretched hand. One cold night he saw the woman lurch and drop the baby. Horrified, he stooped to pick it up—only to discover that it was a rag doll and that the "mother" was dead drunk. He also had taken Christmas baskets to needy families and more than once had met other donors on the doorstep, while meantime needier families were perhaps going hungry. In those days of private charity there were, said Riis, many "preposterous frauds" among the poor. Today, he said, "Charity . . . no longer means alms, but justice."

The better housing, better schools, and small parks now available to the poor were a constant delight to Riis—especially the parks. In his first fifteen years as police reporter on Mulberry Street, before there were any parks, he said that he had never known a week without a murder in the area, while in the five years following the opening of Mulberry Bend Park he had been called only twice to a scene of violence in the Bend.

Riis was careful in his lectures around the country not to confine himself to the changing conditions in New York City. By reading, correspondence, and personal visits he kept up with the social progress in all the major cities of America and, to a lesser degree, with that in European cities. He wrote articles about the situation in St. Louis, Helena, Montana, and Washington, D.C., making practical suggestions. In speaking, he would often repeat, "Neighbor—that is all there is to it," and one could see the familiar twinkle in the blue eyes behind the heavy glasses and the quick smile beneath the droopy gray mustache.

Riis especially enjoyed speaking at colleges and preparatory schools. He was a welcome lecturer at Harvard, Ann Arbor, Oberlin, and Stanford, as well as at Groton and St. Paul's. He had plenty to say to young people and the knack of saying it in a way that gained their attention and aroused their interest in social problems. Quoting Theodore Roosevelt, he would advise them to "Hit the line hard; don't foul, and don't shirk!" He told them that as thinking persons and as American citizens, as well as because the country's future lay in their hands, they should

143

learn all they could about its government—national, state, and city. "A citizen's duty is one thing that cannot be farmed out safely," he warned. "Politics is the weapon," and "Only a fool washes his hands of politics."

Riis urged young people not to take a placid approach toward civic matters. The eternal vigilance that has been called the price of liberty and of the preservation of the state meant, he said, "to sit up with a club"—not to "lay about with it" unnecessarily, but to "keep a firm grip on it." He advised his young listeners "to fight, not to plead, for their rights," and he implored each of them to become so filled "with love of his country and pride in its traditions that he is bound to take the right stand when the time comes." For, he declared solemnly, "Whether for good or for evil, we all leave our mark upon our day."

On his many visits to college campuses, Jacob Riis was never in the least embarrassed in the presence of college presidents or professors, or troubled by his own lack of formal education. In 1904, there was talk about his being given an honorary doctor's degree. He refused vigorously. "Don't you dare 'doctor' me!" he wrote a friend. "I never had a title and I would not know what to do with it." Seriously he added, "It could in no way help the cause I have at heart." But when the Playground and Recreational Association of America was founded in 1906, it made Jacob Riis a lifetime Honorary Vice President. And in 1912 he was made a member of the National Institute of Social Sciences "in recognition of distinction attained by your Philanthropy."

Always responsive to natural beauty, Jacob Riis was delighted with the new interest women's clubs and chambers of commerce were taking in beautifying their cities and towns. The reaction of the slum-dwellers to his flowers, years before, had convinced him of the need for natural beauty in crowded places and shown him how it improved human relations.

Riis approved heartily of the Boy Scouts of America, organized in New York in 1910. He wrote an article about the association in the *Outlook*, predicting that it would give the boys an outlet for their "primitive instincts" and break down barriers of race and creed. At a rally in a New York armory he watched boys pitch camp, wigwag, tie up strained ankles, build fires without matches. "Every boy has in him a little savage and a potential good citizen," he commented. "He would rather be good than bad, all things being even. But they are not even. Give him the street and the gutter for a playground, rob him of his play, and he joins the gang or learns the lessons that do not lead to respect for authority or property. . . . Put before him the other alternative and he will adopt the Scout Law to be dutiful, obedient, helpful, and clean with the same enthusiasm."

Because of his special concern in stamping out tuberculosis, Jacob Riis was tremendously interested when he read that in Europe outdoor treatment in sea air had been discovered to be a cure for children suffering from tuberculosis of the bone. New York City built a small demonstration hospital on a strip of shore at Rockaway Beach. Treatment there proved to be amazingly successful, but it distressed Riis that the Sea Breeze Hospital could handle only forty-five children while nearly five thousand children in the city alone needed attention. Most of these cases were in the tenement district for, as Riis explained, "They are the underfed, badly housed ones into whose

soft bones the germ of tuberculosis makes its way, causing hip disease, ankle-joint disease, decay of the spinal
column, and like ailments, wasting and painful beyond
belief."

Riis's concern led him to spend several days at Sea
Breeze not long after his first wife's death, and then to
write an article about the need for enlarging the hospital.
The Rockefellers, Mrs. Andrew Carnegie, and other
wealthy persons responded with large gifts. At Riis's suggestion President and Mrs. Roosevelt paid a visit to the
hospital, and the press report of this brought in many
contributions, both large and small. Riis was optimistic
that the necessary money to enlarge the hospital would
be raised for, he wrote, this was surely God's work "to
be done by human hands," and everyone must agree that
"children on crutches, or strapped to boards to hold their
backs rigid, were not a good substitute for squirming,
playing, healthy boys and girls." As he went on dramatiz-
ing and publicizing the activity, various organizations got
behind the project, and in time the city took over property needed for the larger hospital. At length, in 1914,
building began.

Another activity in which Riis was deeply involved
was the Fresh Air Summer Camp of the Riis Neighborhood House. It was located on Twin Island in the Pelham
Bay area of Long Island Sound, where the city had contributed a shoreside park and the use of an empty old
mansion. During the summer the Neighborhood House
arranged to take mothers and little children out of the
crowded city to enjoy the natural surroundings of fields,
rocks, grass, and trees at Twin Island. At first, said Riis,
the children, used to city sights and sounds, did not know

what to make of it all and "felt as if they were in a strange country." But soon they relaxed and went skipping about, singing and happily gathering flowers. Over the weekends fathers and older brothers were also welcome, and one bright day, to Riis's delight, President and Mrs. Roosevelt sailed across the Sound to see the city children enjoying the Twin Island camp.

A year after his remarriage Jacob Riis took his second wife and his son Billy to Denmark. He had a triple purpose: to introduce Mary to his family and friends, to get material for articles and perhaps a book with Danish background, and to try to find help for his troublesome heart at one of the noted German spas. In Copenhagen, King Frederick, who had been Crown Prince for most of his life and was now ruler of Denmark, following the death of old King Christian, invited Riis to dinner. Riis, unfortunately, was not well enough to accept the royal invitation.

From the spa Riis wrote his settlement friends that the bath treatments were helping him. "The doctor says the real benefit will come after, if I am careful. That, he says, I must always be hereafter, unless I wish to suffer excruciating pain, which I don't. The trouble is that my heart is greatly enlarged, and they think it half a miracle that I am not a dreadful invalid now. I am not. I am as free from pain as a baby, and in it the doctors find hope that my heart may yet shrink to normal size, it being a very good and serviceable heart, all considered."

Two years later Riis and his wife and son returned to Europe. This time Riis was well enough to allow them to visit several European countries as well as Denmark, where he collected material for a book on Scandinavian heroes. He went again to the German spa and after his return to America followed the spa treatment with a two-week "aftercure" in the Canadian woods.

Out of these two European trips came a dozen articles and eventually two books. *The Old Town* was a collection of stories and reminiscences about Ribe. The other book was a collection of *Hero Tales of the Far North*. Neither of these, however, attained anything like the popularity of *How the Other Half Lives* and *The Making of an American*. But a discerning reviewer said of *The Old Town:* "It has a double charm, the charm that is associated with an old place shut off from the world's main currents, and the charm of showing the origins of an interesting personality. . . . It is a book of the heart."

17
Pine Brook Farm

"I would not have missed being in
it all for anything."

—The Making of an American

For years Jacob Riis had wanted a place in the country. The summer after he and Elisabeth celebrated their silver wedding anniversary they looked for one in the gentle Berkshire mountains of western Massachusetts, but property values were too high for them. Now, ten years later, with more money saved from lecturing and writing and with a heart dictating a much quieter way of life, Jacob and Mary Riis renewed the search.

Both of them believed they could make a Berkshire farm—the right Berkshire farm—not only a country home but a paying investment. They would grow fruit and potatoes ("because everybody eats") and raise sheep ("because I like them"). After several discouraging inspections of run down farms and sagging farmhouses, they found their dream farm. It was two hundred acres on a hilltop called Crown Hill, with a hundred-year-old farmhouse "perfectly simple but with noble lines and sound timbers." The slopes were ideal for growing fruit, the soil good for vegetables, and the brook alive with trout. They consulted the "agricultural sharps" at the state farm college and, after getting their approval,

149

bought the place. Happily Riis declared, "I see peace and prosperity abiding on Crown Hill forevermore."

They named it Pine Brook Farm and began the necessary renovations. In the summer of 1912, as changes were made in the house, they lived in tents set up in a nearby field. While barns, sheds, and fences were being built, they bought horses, cattle, and pigs (Riis does not mention sheep!), tools and seeds, had a well dug and land cleared. Mary Riis became expert in making wise investments that, with time, could turn the property into a self-supporting farm. Jacob Riis used his carpentry skill to build a potato cellar out of an old cider mill. He reveled in it all, hating to leave it even long enough to make two brief trips to New York during the summer.

In a two-part article published in the *Craftsman* in the fall of 1913, Riis describes the Berkshire farm and tells of their early days there. He writes humorously of their troubles—the witchgrass, the bugs, the drought, the frosts, foxes killing chickens, geese eating lettuce, cows munching green tomatoes, "Lady-horse" demonstrating that she had a mind of her own. In such a spot, he asks, "Who could grow old in heart?" Certainly not Jacob Riis! I am "glad that the lengthening shadows find me in this place with my feet on the soil to which my dust shall return," he writes, and he describes the view over the valley from their front door—a view that included the arched "gateway into the garden of the dead, the God's acre of those whose work is done."

In New York, although the mortgage had been paid off on the enlarged Riis Neighborhood House and birds were singing in its roof garden, funds were still needed to finance various activities, including summer outings for small children and their mothers. This, added to the heavy investments in Pine Brook Farm, made Riis insist on going on with his lecture tours, though he admitted that traveling and lecturing were harder for him than they had been. He wanted to be useful and to continue to promote the causes he believed in so strongly. His health seemed pretty good; for nearly two years he had had hardly any serious trouble with his heart.

Magazine articles flowed from his pen—articles about the farm, about Denmark, and forward-looking pieces on current social problems. His concern about public health was shown by an article warning of the risk involved in permitting "contract tailoring"—the current term for sweatshops. Buyers of garments made or partly made in tenement homes, he wrote, still ran the chance of contracting scarlet fever, diphtheria, or some other contagious disease. It was quite possible for a disease to go unreported, or for a worker to disregard safeguards. He went so far as to state: "Contract work in tenements must be forbidden entirely."

Looking ahead, Riis advocated antipollution measures, the widening of streets, the construction of more playgrounds, and the building of still more schools. These he would like to see named after great men instead of being given numbers.

Roosevelt, having been out of the White House for a term while William Howard Taft was President, bolted his Republican party to organize a third party that he called the Progressives. As always, Riis supported his friend. He even made a few campaign speeches for him while on lecture tours in the Middle West and in the South. And he was deeply disappointed when "Teddy" failed to win the 1912 election.

Early in December, Riis covered the second National Housing Association convention in Philadelphia for his old paper, the *New York Sun*. When his report was later reprinted in the *Survey*, it was accompanied by this editorial note: "Mr. Riis's lifelong battle against the slum has made him perhaps the one man in America best qualified to catch and interpret the spirit of this meeting." In summarizing the progress made in some of the seventy-six cities represented at the convention, Riis mentioned the tearing down of old tenements, the variety being introduced in new housing, the increased cooperation with city departments, provision of adequate sewage, and the outlawing of alley houses, with their high infant mortality. He quoted significant statements of different speakers: "Bigness is no cause for pride; only fitness is." And "The health of the people is the test of civilization."

That Christmas of 1912, Riis helped arrange the details of erecting a Christmas tree in Manhattan's Madison Square. This may have been the first American outdoor community Christmas tree. And on New Year's Eve he was responsible for managing a huge "sing" around the tree. "I invented it all," he said happily. "I was stage manager and even 'bossed' the music!" As a finale the crowd sang "Auld Lang Syne" and taps were played on a trumpet. To Riis's delight these seemed to outdo the sound of horns welcoming in the New Year.

Keeping up two establishments—Richmond Hill in winter, Pine Brook Farm in summer—proved to be too expensive, so, early in 1913, the Riises gave up their Long

Island home. Hereafter, Jacob Riis announced, his legal residence would be Massachusetts rather than New York. But he continued to be involved in many New York projects, and his correspondence from the Berkshires was extremely heavy.

"He never spared himself in writing," a friend later testified. "Often because of the drain on his strength he was urged not to handle them all [incoming letters], but he used to clear his desk every day." He wrote often to the Riis Neighborhood House to give advice, to New York City Hall to protest cuts in certain appropriations he felt were essential, to state legislators to recommend setting up a farm colony and enacting various progressive measures; to civic leaders to urge a campaign against Tammany; and to friends—"wonderful letters," one of the friends said, "full of gaiety and the philosophy of life." Full, too, of "courage, practical suggestions, enthusiasm—whether to a group of college boys or a civic league in some out-of-the-way village, or a railroad president with a social outlook."

Riis's output of articles kept up, chiefly in the *Outlook, Century, Craftsman,* and *Independent.* His 1913 spring lecture program was shorter than it had been in previous years and it was with real relief that he finished it and returned for a long summer at Pine Brook Farm.

It was a happy summer in spite of a return of his heart trouble. The farm was gradually being turned into a modern, self-supporting enterprise. Billy was home from nearby Williams College. Mrs. Riis's mother, of whom they were all very fond, was with them, and John and his wife came for a visit.

In late June, Riis wrote his settlement staff: "I am feeling better today than for quite a while, and am altogether on the upgrade, I believe. Poor stick at the best, I feel selfish and mean being up here with all of you down in New York struggling with the summer problems. But as my wife says truly, I wouldn't be any use there, for I would collapse at once. So I stay. Good luck to you ever."

By October, Riis was well enough to give a talk at a meeting of the Massachusetts Teachers Association and to speak at several New England schools and colleges. With the coming of chill winds and freezing temperatures, the Berkshire farm became too cold for comfort, so the Riises rented an apartment in Manhattan for the winter months. Despite Jacob Riis's distaste for city living, being in New York had many advantages. He could easily keep in touch with his New York friends and the various organizations with which he was actively connected, most of all with the Riis Neighborhood House.

During the winter, Riis undertook a lecture tour to the Middle West. His wife tried to dissuade him, but he insisted, saying, "It will hurt me more to give up those lectures, I think, if I can make them at all, than to try." But in the middle of the tour he had to take time out for a rest at the Battle Creek Sanitarium in Michigan. Against advice he started out again, going to Illinois, on to Texas, and then to Louisiana. In New Orleans he collapsed.

With difficulty Riis made the long trip north to Battle Creek and there had an attack of bronchitis that was almost fatal. "Now that I have to fight for almost every breath of air," he said, "I am more thankful than ever that I have been instrumental in helping the children of the tenements to obtain fresh air." He would not give up.

From his sickbed, while fighting for life, he dictated letters and telegrams.

Mary Riis and Billy came on from Massachusetts and with their help Jacob Riis made the trip back to Pine Brook Farm. He collapsed when nearly there, but seemed better for a short time after reaching home. Then he had a relapse and weakened. On May 25, 1914, he died.

The simple home funeral service was conducted by his friend Dr. Endicott Peabody, headmaster of Groton School for Boys. There were no flowers; an announcement stated: "The family desires to carry out the wish of the deceased that no flowers be sent to his funeral and that such money be rather expended on more needy objects." The burial was, as he had wished, in the little "God's acre" near the farm. There four Groton boys sang a few of Jacob Riis's favorite hymns. It was only a few months earlier that he had written: "In my happy valley I would live, and here I would lie, a weary toiler, glad of his rest when the day's tasks are done." By his request the grave was marked by a granite field boulder, with no inscription. His life, he believed, should speak for him.

Jacob Riis, the man who had wanted to wear out, not to rust, had almost literally worn himself out working to better the lives of others. The last article published before his death was a plea, in the May 9 *Outlook,* for the Sea Breeze tubercular children's hospital. A piece by him appeared in *Playground* the following year, prefaced by this statement: "Mr. Riis was, at the time of his death, engaged upon the preparation of an article on the play movement for one of the news syndicates. This paper represents the beginning of the uncompleted plan and is probably the last writing he did."

Although a humble man, Jacob Riis could hardly have helped being proud of what was said and written about him after his death. "I feel as if I had lost an own brother," wired Theodore Roosevelt. "Jake's friendship has meant more to me than I can ever say." And he wrote: "He was one of my truest and closest friends. I have loved him dearly and I mourn him as if he were one of my own family."

The Danish legation in Washington extolled Jacob Riis's "untiring and self-sacrificing work for the good of the poor and the distinguished position which he had won for himself in this country [that] reflected great credit also on his native land."

At a meeting of the Intercity Settlement Conference, held in New York soon after Riis's death, Dr. Jane Robbins spoke with feeling of his lifework, and Lillian Wald presented a resolution that mentioned his "genius for friendship and for intelligent sympathy born of his remarkable capacity for happy, playful comradeship." Millions, the resolution went on, were affected by the influence of this man who, with his love of humanity, saw the needs of the forgotten dwellers in the great cities, and "opened up the hearts of a people to emotion and the knowledge upon which to guide this emotion into effective channels."

On a more personal note his wife Mary wrote a friend: "Surely the candle he lighted must burn always until it lights the darkness in uncounted lives to come. There was something so shining about him. He was good but he was more than good—radiantly, gloriously good, and so adorably human always."

156

18

"The Living Heritage of Jacob Riis"

"Whether for good or evil, we all
leave our mark upon our day."
—*Theodore Roosevelt, the Citizen*

Skip thirty-five years from the placing of the unmarked granite boulder in the little Berkshire "garden of the dead." It is 1949 and time to celebrate the hundred-year anniversary of Jacob Riis's birth. Who will remember?

The Mayor of New York, the Honorable William O'Dwyer, declares May 1 to May 8 to be Jacob Riis Week—seven days dedicated to honoring "the father of slum clearance" and commemorating the memory of "New York's most useful citizen."

On the evening of his birthday, May 3, there is a testimonial dinner at the Waldorf-Astoria. (One recalls Riis's first newspaper assignment when, almost starving, he reported a luncheon at the Astor.) The dinner is sponsored jointly by the Citizens Housing and Planning Council of New York and the Jacob A. Riis Neighborhood Settlement—still going strong more than half a century after its founding. Eleanor Roosevelt, one of the speakers, says

157

that, if Jacob Riis were living today, he would be pointing out not the fears but the strength of our democracy.

In Ribe, Denmark, also on May 3, "thousands of Danes gathered before the house where Jacob Riis was born . . . to pay homage to his memory." Among them was a sister (Sophie), journalists, and representatives from various Danish organizations and from the United States embassy.

An editorial in the *New York Times* pays tribute to Jacob Riis, citing the words of Theodore Roosevelt: "He had a passion for righteousness," and attributing to him "a gift for making people ashamed of themselves when they deserved to be." It mentions his "battle for good housing, for decent shelters for the homeless, for parks and playgrounds, for schools as neighborhood centers, for pure drinking water," and says that he "startled a complacent New York into a sense of responsibility on slum conditions." Because of Jacob Riis, "public and official attitude is now far more enlightened." His memory, the editorial ends, still holds "a challenge and an inspiration."

Most impressive of the centenary tributes is a lengthy article by Robert Moses, New York City Park Commissioner. Published in the Sunday magazine section of the *New York Times*, it is titled: "The Living Heritage of Jacob Riis," with a line beneath reading: "What he thought and did still affects the city and many of us continue to live by his ideals."

In a "dog-eat-dog, devil-take-the-hindmost era" this first-generation American, says Mr. Moses, "committed himself to the proposition that man is his brother's keeper, that the lives of the other half are the concern of the upper crust, and that prosperity based on human misery is a delusion."

Among Jacob Riis's "countless" reforms Mr. Moses lists the destruction of rear tenements, the construction of playgrounds and parks, child labor laws, good schools, pure water, and the regulation of housing and health by law. It took a long time, says Mr. Moses, but at last the lesson sank in that "these things are a first and continuing obligation of any decent municipal government, not to be left to charity or chance political handouts." Riis's influence, says Mr. Moses, spread to other cities, and his reforms "were elevated to accepted standards by which municipal decency was measured everywhere."

Calling Jacob Riis "an American, deep and undiluted," Mr. Moses echoes Theodore Roosevelt's words: "the nearest to being the ideal American." He declares that Riis has not been forgotten and prays: "May his shadow never grow less."

This belated acknowledgment of the debt municipal governments owe Jacob Riis is satisfying. But what of the average citizen? How is he obligated to Riis and what cause has he to remember this Danish-born "deep and undiluted" American?

To consider Jacob Riis solely responsible for all the social reform that took place at the beginning of the twentieth century would be an exaggeration. The years of Riis's police reporting on Mulberry Street were years that saw a great upsurge of interest in social problems. It was the right time for an able and concerned journalist to raise his voice to rouse a generally apathetic public to the plight of the people of the slums. Riis's was not a solitary voice, but it was a powerful one, probably the most powerful of the time, and it grew ever more forceful, ever more effective.

Some of Riis's ideas and methods were criticized as being oversimple, sentimental, idealistic. Critics said he exaggerated the evils of the slum, of the police lodging-room system, of the courts and jails. His notion that childhood was a time for play seemed preposterous to parents who regarded children as economic assets. Why should their children not work for them as they, most of them, had worked for their parents? That the long hours and bad air and occasional accidents in factories would take their toll was a fact of life to be expected. Nor did "sweaters" appreciate this busy little man's efforts to increase inspections, or dishonest politicians approve his struggle to clean up corruption.

Yet when the changes he advocated eventually came about and good came of them, many of the very ones who had called Riis's ideas foolish or fanatical began to label them progressive. Here, they began to say, was a man who worked for the good of the people, a wise and farsighted man, a man ahead of his time.

In the matter of housing—Riis's major concern—no one could deny he was the one chiefly responsible for bringing about improvements that resulted in a drastic drop in death, disease, and crime rates in New York's poor districts. Year by year housing standards were raised until, when Mr. Moses wrote in the mid-twentieth century, they had reached the commonly accepted high level of "low-income" apartment complexes, many of them financed by the city. Bearing witness to this and named in honor of the man who did so much to start it all, Mr. Moses could point to the Riis Houses, a huge project along New York's East River, with comfortable, desirable apartments and well-designed architecture and landscaping, and distinguished by the nationally acclaimed Riis Plaza. Nor do Riis Houses stand alone; comparable developments exist in other American cities. Whatever slums still stand, bad though they may be judged by today's standards, they cannot be compared with the intolerable tenements of Riis's day.

In modern terms Jacob Riis might be called an antipollution fighter and the slum clearance he worked for an antipollution measure. When Mulberry Bend was demolished, some said its poison and poverty would just be scattered. Not so, said Riis. "The slum itself is the poison." Its air, he said, was "fouler than the mud of the gutter." He might appropriately have used a term Ralph Nader used in 1971 when he spoke of a certain slum district as a "pollution-intense" area.

In other ways besides replacing the disease-ridden slum tenements with decent buildings with open spaces did Riis prove himself a champion of public health. He warned against danger from contagious diseases in sweatshops; he fought tuberculosis, then a top killer, by introducing the Danish Christmas stamps that became the National Tuberculosis Christmas seals; he helped to promote health habits in the tenements and in schools.

Education, too, found a champion in Jacob Riis. He worked for it on all levels—kindergartens for the little ones (an ultra "progressive" idea at the time), more and better elementary schools, trade schools for older boys and girls, adult education (also a "new" idea). He encouraged the formation of clubs and lecture courses at settlements and was one of the founders of the People's

Institute for popular education at New York's Cooper Union. Education, Riis realized, was essential for the thousands of immigrants who arrived in New York "too helpless to strike out for themselves." These foreign-born people needed many different kinds of help in order to learn how to help themselves. Settlements did much; so did Riis as an individual. "The slightest push, the lift of a finger at the right time is sometimes enough to start a family that hovers on the edge of pauperism on the road to independence," he wrote. No one will ever know to how many families Riis gave that push, thus putting them "on the road to independence."

Jacob Riis is rightfully honored as the "father of the small park movement," the initiator of today's "vest-pocket" parks. By insistent "nagging" at city officials he succeeded in getting many small parks in the crowded area where there had not been a single "spot of green." City school playgrounds, too, were due to Riis, who almost single-handedly pushed through the New York State Legislature the law that "no school shall be built without an adequate playground." He did not live to see Randall's Island turned into a municipal park and playground—a project he had urged. But a popular beach playground now bears his name—a stretch of sandy shore on Rockaway Beach called the Jacob A. Riis Park in honor of his lifelong fight for parks for the people. It was Riis who had prodded the city into buying the land, but its naming came at the time of his death as a suggestion from Theodore Roosevelt and others.

All his life Riis practiced his belief that journalism should be used to promote good citizenship. He had a great faith in the power of the press—a faith he justified many times.

Riis had great faith in the power of women, too, at a time when this was a radical idea. In the struggle for school reform in New York it was women, he said, who "struck the telling blows." He gave them credit as well for often doing better than men in the delicate job of nudging through the state legislature some important bill. Along with his high regard for women's ability in public life, Riis held, perhaps inconsistently, a rather sentimental, old-fashioned notion of women, putting them on a pedestal, sometimes to the amusement of his more cynical fellow reporters.

But they never laughed at his touching concern for children, individually and collectively. While most people of his day did not hesitate to herd orphans and unwanted children into asylums, Riis contended that children belonged in homes, not in institutions. He worked hard and wrote many articles to promote this idea.

Above all, it was Riis's passion for justice, in place of charity, that inspired most of his busy, fighting lifetime. "Society exists for the purpose of securing justice for its members," he wrote. If only the poor were given justice, Riis believed with all his heart that they would live up to their opportunities, and that the world would be a better place.

Jacob Riis's many contributions to the betterment of American life, especially for the poor, include more than housing, parks, schools, pure water, child-labor laws. He was important, too, as the first documentary reporter-photographer, the initiator of human-interest newspaper stories. His life in his adopted country fairly overflowed with deeds of significance.

Water, however, rises no higher than its source, or deeds than the character of the doer. Jacob Riis's stature— his courage, his persistence, his optimism, and his "cheerful, fighting spirit" will not be forgotten. Nor will the importance of a life spent for others, seeking to "reform by humane touch" and to secure for the poor "not charity, but justice."

BOOKS BY JACOB A. RIIS

How the Other Half Lives   (Scribner, 1890)
Children of the Poor   (Scribner, 1892)
Out of Mulberry Street   (Century, 1898)
A Ten Years' War   (Houghton, 1900)
The Making of an American   (Macmillan, 1901)
The Battle with the Slum   (Macmillan, 1902)
Children of the Tenements   (Macmillan, 1903)
The Peril and Preservation of the Home   (Jacobs, 1903)
Is There a Santa Claus?   (Macmillan, 1904)
Theodore Roosevelt, the Citizen   (Macmillan, 1904)
The Old Town   (Macmillan, 1909)
Neighbors   (Macmillan, 1914)
Hero Tales of the Far North   (Macmillan, 1919)
Christmas Stories   (Macmillan, 1923)

A
Selected
Bibliography

In addition to Mr. Riis's own books we suggest:

Cordasco, Francesco, ed. *Jacob Riis Revisited: Poverty and the Slum in Another Era* (Abridgments of Jacob Riis's *How the Other Half Lives, The Children of the Poor,* and *A Ten Years' War*) (Doubleday Anchor Books, 1968)

Ford, James *Slums and Housing, with special reference to New York City History. Conditions. Policy* (2 vols. Harvard University Press, 1936)

Hapgood, Hutchins and Golden, Harry *The Spirit of the Ghetto: Studies of the Jewish Quarter of New York,* with Jacob Epstein drawings (revised ed. 1965. Funk & Wagnalls, 1902)

Harrington, Michael *The Other America: Poverty in the United States* (Macmillan, 1962)

Holmes, John Haynes "Jacob August Riis"—in *Dictionary of American Biography*

Museum of the City of New York. Byron Collection *New York as Photographed by Byron and Described by Grace M. Mayer* (Macmillan, 1958)

A Selected Bibliography

Rischin, Moses *The Promised City: New York's Jews, 1870–1914* (Harvard University Press, 1962)

Roosevelt, Theodore *An Autobiography* (Macmillan, 1916)

Schoener, Allon, ed. *Portal to America—The Lower East Side 1870–1925* (Holt, 1967)

Steffens, Lincoln *Autobiography* (Harcourt, 1937)

Wald, Lillian B. *The House on Henry Street* (Holt, 1915)

Ware, Louise *Jacob A. Riis: Police Reporter, Reformer, Useful Citizen* (Appleton-Century, 1938)

Index

169